the definitive guide to
project management

the fast track to getting the job done
on time and on budget

Sebastian Nokes, Ian Major, Alan Greenwood,
Dominic Allen, Mark Goodman

FT Prentice Hall
FINANCIAL TIMES

An imprint of **Pearson Education**

London • New York • Toronto • Sydney • Tokyo • Singapore
Hong Kong • Cape Town • Madrid • Paris • Amsterdam • Munich • Milan

PEARSON EDUCATION LIMITED

Head Office:
Edinburgh Gate
Harlow CM20 2JE
Tel: +44 (0)1279 623623
Fax: +44 (0)1279 431059

website: www.pearsoned.co.uk

_____

First published in Great Britain in 2003

ISBN 0 273 66397 6

British Library Cataloguing in Publication Data
A CIP catalogue record for this book can be obtained from the British Library

10 9 8 7 6 5 4 3 2 1

Typeset by Northern Phototypesetting Co. Ltd, Bolton
Printed and bound in Great Britain by Bell and Bain Ltd, Glasgow

The Publishers' policy is to use paper manufactured from sustainable forests.

about the authors

SEBASTIAN NOKES

Sebastian is chairman of Project Value Associates Ltd, a leading project management advisory firm. Sebastian was trained in project management at IBM and in the Royal Air Force. He has led many projects in the capital markets, technology and publishing sectors. When working at Credit Suisse First Boston, Sebastian led a number of major projects and was part of the team that updated the bank's approach to project management. He has managed projects for a number of investment and commercial banks and the UK government. Within project management he specializes in planning and work breakdown structure. Sebastian has a BA in Philosophy and an MSc in Finance from London University and is a member of the IEEE. He may be contacted at Nokes@ITVA.net

IAN MAJOR

Ian is a director of Project Value Associates Ltd, a leading project management advisory firm. Ian was trained in project management at Coopers & Lybrand and at IBM. He has led many projects in the industrial, capital markets, retail financial and technology sectors. He is also an experienced project sponsor and has held senior management positions in Midland Montagu (now HSBC), IBM and Scient. At Midland Ian was Financial Engineering Director. At IBM he led the growth of consulting revenue. Within project management he specializes in programme governance, project sponsorship and project risk management. Ian has a BSc in Economics from Bristol University, he is a Fellow of the Chartered Institute of Management Accountants and he was a member of the Association of Corporate Treasurers.

ALAN GREENWOOD

Alan is an experienced project manager and a regular lecturer on project management for Project Value Associates Ltd. He has a BSc in psychology and an MBA from London Business School.

MARK GOODMAN

Mark Goodman has many years' project management experience gained in both the public and private sectors. He has led projects at BT, NTL, Barclays Bank and previously while serving in the British Army. Mark has a BA from Oxford Polytechnic and an MBA from Cranfield.

contents

List of figures

Checklists

Cases

preface

Your organization will succeed in its ambitions to survive and grow if it is successful in managing change. In order to survive it must change in response to the changing market environment, and, in order to grow, it must initiate change proactively as well as responsively.

Projects are the means to bring about change, whether it is large or small. They are the means to get things done which are not part of current day-to-day activities. Hence, projects are key to the future of an organization. It is imperative that you identify, select and deliver the right projects in the most efficient way.

Project managers are a vital part of this process. The organization depends on them at all stages of a project, from defining what it will do, through selecting the right project, delivering projects with maximum benefits, to ensuring that learning is captured. Success in turning change into a competitive weapon depends on project managers.

This book is intended to help project managers achieve consistently high standards in everything they do. It does not replace experience or common sense, but it does provide a convenient single reference source to lock in good practice, jog memory, reduce time spent searching for guidance, and help avoid known pitfalls. Project managers should keep this guide on hand and make use of it continuously.

Part I
background information

1

introduction

▶ Imagine . . .

Imagine yourself one Sunday afternoon a few months from now. This particular Sunday afternoon is one just like any other over the past nine weeks; you have been at the office all weekend and the chances of getting away before dark are slim. There is just too much to do. You know that the stress will not end even when you get home. The weeks of not doing your share of the domestic tasks are beginning to strain relationships. What started as understanding and support for the pressure you are under is now wearing very thin. You cannot even comfort yourself that your exceptional commitment will be recognized in your annual assessment next year. Your boss is hardly likely to give you a good review for all this work when he or she she is the one who said what a waste of time it was in the first place.

This scenario is not fictional. It is not even unusual. It is an everyday story of a project manager in trouble. If you are reading this before taking on your first project management position, you should be aware that you really could find yourself in this situation a few months from now. The techniques described in this book will help you avoid such situations. Projects can be managed, and managed in a way that keeps your life in balance as well as delivering business benefits on time and on budget. The skills required are well within the capabilities of most professionals if they take the trouble to learn and apply them. But few do, and this is why the picture painted above is so common; without the right skills projects can all too easily turn into nightmares.

In an alternative version of the future, you have learned and applied the methods set out in this book. Maybe it took some additional effort at the beginning to go through the book rather than to launch straight in with the work, but with hindsight you know it was worthwhile. Managing a project that is going well is a good feeling. Having your predictions about something as notoriously unpredictable as a project proved right is very satisfying. Even problems can be gratifying since you may find that you have predicted them and have solutions prepared. Being associated with success is a fantastic morale booster for everyone on the team, and your reputation with team members and people across the organization will be exceptional. With such a reputation, future projects will be easier, and you may begin to have influence over which projects you and the firm wish to undertake.

▶ About this book

This book is made up of four main sections:

1 The first describes the role that projects play in organizations and provides a framework of project management processes and generic project phases around which the rest of the book is structured.

2 The second covers the basic principles that should govern how projects are run.

3 The third describes each of the project management processes that must be applied through the life of a project.

4 The fourth describes in detail what should happen in each phase of a project.

Much of project management is common sense but in some areas it involves special tools or methods that must be learned. There is a variety of such methods some of which are mutually incompatible and attempting to describe them all is likely to cause confusion. Rather than risk confusion this book has been written to reflect just one: the critical chain method. Projects managed using the critical chain method have been shown to have a far greater chance of delivering the required outputs on time and on budget than those managed any other way. The critical chain method is significantly different from the project planning and control methods taught on project management courses until recently, and it may therefore be new learning even for experienced project managers. For the benefit of those seeking an overview there is a separate description of critical chain and its rationale in Appendix A.

It has been assumed that most of the readers of this book will be people who are just starting their project management career and who work in an organization where there is already a framework for handling projects. Some readers may not be part of any such organization either because they are sole traders or because their organization does not yet know about projects. In either case, a little common-sense reinterpretation may be required but this book can be valuable because it outlines the framework that has been shown to work successfully in many other organizations.

This book provides a single reference source for project managers. It provides guidance for project managers in all key aspects of project management. By applying the learning from this book, a project manager should be able to define, plan and execute a small or medium-sized project, identifying and managing deviations from plans as required. The same skills are applicable to managing portions of larger projects. Nevertheless, there are two important limitations on how this book should be used:

◆ Though some aspects of project management can be formalized in a book, much of what matters must be learned through experience. Nobody should be placed in the position of having to run their first project using only a book for support. People who are new to project management may make more use of this book, but they should also make full use of the support available from experienced colleagues and from the project support department within their firm.

◆ Almost by definition, projects involve tackling new problems. This means that sometimes, a project will encounter a problem which does not fit logically into the framework outlined in this book. It is essential that we remember that books are not a substitute for common sense: if there are sound reasons for doing things differently to the way presented here, then do things differently. This is not to say that the framework presented here has no value, but rather that common sense is more valuable still.

The framework presented here is relatively loose, and fits best with the small and medium-sized projects that are by far the most likely to be encountered by people starting out in project management. Large projects are more demanding, and usually require more structure and formal procedures just to keep them under control. Such formal project management tools are exemplified by the PRINCE 2® method, which is widely recognized as a benchmark in project management methods (PRINCE 2 is a trademark of the Central Computer and Telecommunications Agency in the UK). The PRINCE 2 method can be overlaid on the framework outlined here, but it includes extensions, while essential for large complex projects, do not materially add value to small projects. So most project managers will find the framework given here applicable most of the time, but managers of large and complex projects should consider adding in the additional processes outlined in PRINCE 2 or another formal method.

Fig. 1.1 Project difficulty

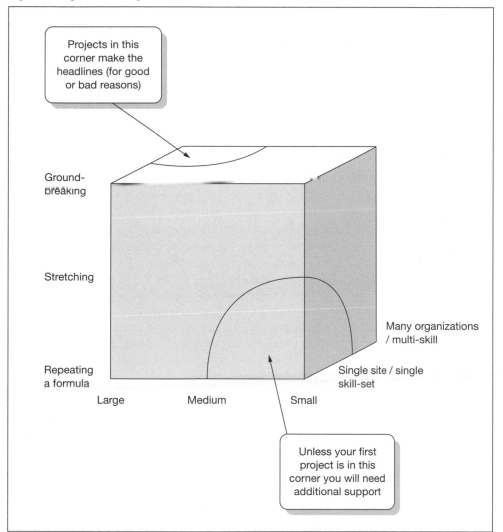

For convenience, we classify projects as small, medium or large. But this is not the only criterion that should be applied when assessing the degree of difficulty in managing a project. It is much easier to manage a project where all the activities are familiar and will take place in the same organization than it is to manage something novel that relies on several different organizations (see Fig. 1.1). The techniques described in this book apply in all circumstances but the challenges of large, complex, risky projects are disproportionately greater, and this is why they should be left for the most experienced project managers.

As well as PRINCE 2, the other widely accepted standard in company procedures is the ISO 9000 series. These do not address projects directly, but instead focus on how to ensure that customers consistently get what they want. Given that so many projects are concerned with creating products for customers or creating processes to get products to customers, the relevance of ISO 9000 to projects should be clear. Nonetheless it would be inappropriate to try to bind this book too closely to the ISO 9000 standards because relatively few organizations have adopted them fully, and because one of the key features of the ISO 9000 standards is the flexibility to adapt them to individual company operations. Companies that have adopted ISO 9000 will certainly have their own procedures and the principles outlined in this book should fit with most of these.

Projects crop up in all sorts of places in all sorts of organizations and many people doubt that it is possible to apply the same techniques of project management to all projects. Is it reasonable to try to manage the development of a blood chemistry analyzer in the same way as the launch of a new credit card? Are either of these the same as an office move? Project management applies in all of these situations because despite their different technical and business domains they all have the same underlying need for structure. That is not to say that someone with no knowledge of clinical chemistry could manage a blood chemistry analyzer project. But the planning and project control techniques used on a blood chemistry analyzer project would be the same as those used on the others. So the scope of this book is not limited to a single technical or business domain. If you still doubt that the project management techniques described in this book can be applied in your domain, read the book. You should not have any problem interpreting what is written here in the context of your work, despite the fact that someone from a completely different sector can also see its relevance to them.

Projects

Projects and processes

Organizations are made up of groups of people doing things. The things they do are varied but everything can be categorized as either a project or a process. This may sound like such a sweeping statement that it cannot possibly be true but it is. Processes are either activities that take place continuously or are a known sequence of operations that are repeated whenever circumstances require. Some types of oil refining plant run continuously day and night and they are a good example of a process. Running a telephone exchange might be an equivalent process for a telecoms company. The exchange equipment runs continuously but phone calls arrive at irregular intervals. The sequence of events associated with the arrival of a phone call is so well defined that the actions have been completely automated.

But some things that happen in organizations are not quite so repeatable, and in these cases the processes need to be adapted. For example, though the procedure for certain sorts of surgical operations are well defined, surgeons must be skilled in adapting the procedure both to the general condition of each patient and to the specific circumstances found once the operation is under way. When a company changes its raw materials suppliers the manufacturing process may be unaffected but if the different suppliers have different grades of material then the process may need to be adapted. So processes can be set up in such a way that they can cope with normal variations in conditions.

But sometimes the adaptation required is such that it takes the process outside the region of previous experience. If the different grade of raw material needed to be treated at a much higher temperature than that from the original supplier, for example, then there would be a risk that the existing equipment would be unable to handle the new material. So before adopting the new material, the company should check the implications of the adoption for their equipment and confirm that the change of material is still economically attractive even after necessary equipment upgrades have been paid for. In other words, the company would run a brief project to study the decision and make sure that the changeover happens smoothly. If the decision is made to adopt the new material and the project is successful then the manufacturing process can continue thereafter. The project changes an existing process (see Fig. 1.2).

Fig. 1.2 Projects and processes

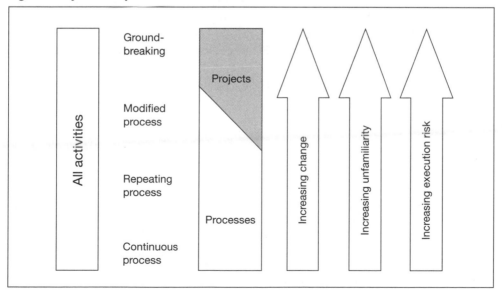

The dividing line between projects and processes depends on whether the organization repeats an activity often enough for it to become routine. For example, a large construction company might build a new housing development consisting of hundreds of near-identical houses. Their process of building a house is very well defined, but there may be different drainage or access requirements at different ends of the site so that the construction methods may be slightly different as a result. For this company, house-building is a process that can be repeated with a little adaptation. But if you were to build your own house, then it would almost certainly be a project. You are very unlikely to be as practised at building houses as the company that builds the housing development.

One way to distinguish between a project and a process in any particular organization is the degree of execution risk involved. Procedures that get repeated frequently are usually refined through experience to the point where they are very unlikely to fail. Thousands of cans of beer pass along a canning line every minute and the likelihood that any particular can will be found to be outside its specified limits is very small. The Six Sigma movement is mostly concerned with this sort of continuous process improvement so that customers always get what they want. But as the novelty of a process increases, so does the risk that it will fail to produce the desired result, and with entirely new ventures there are no pre-existing processes that can be refined. Creating a new process necessarily involves doing new things and discovering the right way to do them necessarily involves making some mistakes. New combinations of technologies or new markets usually mean that the people who have to do the project have not worked together before and there is no pre-existing organizational framework or protocol to guide their interactions. So before ground-breaking projects can begin to achieve their business objectives they must first create a new organization and this is itself fraught with risks. These activities involve such high risk that trying to manage them within the framework of the firm's usual activities is very likely to lead to disaster. A different management approach is needed for these high-risk activities, and this is why project management is different from day-to-day management.

This definition of a project as an activity that brings about change is very broad. Not all activities that fit with this definition get identified as projects and managed accordingly. However, it is not unusual to find that one of the main reasons for failed initiatives and stalled launches is that they were not managed as projects. It does not matter whether the word project is used – it only matters that the proper management techniques are applied.

eg Cisco

The acquisition of another company is a rare event in the life of most organizations. Such an event clearly changes the organization and requires careful planning and execution. It would be a major project in almost any firm.

Cisco, the Internet equipment supplier, grew from $28 million revenues to $8.5 billion in only nine years having deliberately adopted a strategy of growth by acquisition. At one time Cisco was acquiring another firm on average every 16 days!

Acquisitions are notoriously difficult to get right, particularly when the most valuable part of the acquired firm is the people. But Cisco's growth plan required lots of acquisitions, and so one of the four main parts of the plan was to 'systematize the acquisition process'. Rather that reinvent the wheel with every acquisition, Ciso had strict procedures that included things such as:

♦ Standard pre-acquisition criteria and due diligence processes.

♦ A strict timetable for getting acquired companies' supply chains integrated into the Cisco system so that cost savings were immediately realized and the greater reach of the Cisco sales network could increase sales of the acquired company's products.

♦ A formal system of buddying new employees with Cisco employees who had similar experience. The Cisco buddy had specific responsibility for making sure that new joiners knew the Cisco procedures.

♦ Structuring the deal to ensure employee retention and to align motivations of new employees with Cisco.

♦ Appointing a respected senior manager from the acquired company to lead the integration process.

These measures had been proven to address many of the common reasons for failure of company mergers. Cisco repeated the acquisition project so many times that it was able to formalize procedures in a way that greatly improved the speed of company integrations and the chances of success. They had taken what would normally be a rare and risky project and turned it into a routine process.

▶ Your firm depends on project excellence

Most firms' day-to-day operations serve customers through a network of interconnecting business processes. As business volumes change, the loading on these processes can increase or decrease, and, as explained above, there is often some adaptation possible within each process. But it would take the cumulative effect of many adaptations to change the fundamentals of even one of the business processes, and this would take years. Markets change over a period of weeks rather than years, and so firms cannot afford to wait for this gradual adaptation. However, making change happen more rapidly requires effort and resources over and above what is available from people who are already working hard on day-to-day tasks. Projects provide a structure so that people can work to change the firm at a much faster rate than would be possible through cumulative process adaptation. As the rate of change in markets increases and product life cycles shorten, the importance of projects will increase.

One of the roles of projects is to replace old inefficient ways of doing things with methods that are better suited to modern market conditions. Over time a succession of projects completely renew and replace the set of processes used in a firm's day-to-day operations. So the quality of the fit between the firm's processes and the needs of the market depends on the quality of its projects. Projects that take too long leave the firm with out-of-date products or capabilities, and projects that deliver low-quality results soon lead to lower sales. So the future of the firm really does depend on its projects. As markets change more quickly and become more demanding the pressure on projects will increase.

Fig. 1.3 Successful projects improve the firm

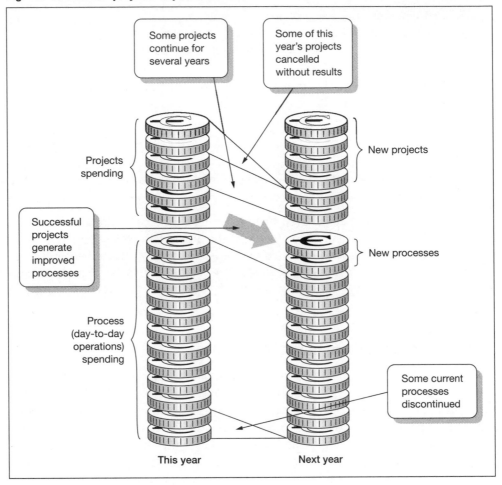

The pressure on projects becomes greater still when we remember that it is only the successful projects that give rise to new processes. In many organizations up to one-third of projects are cancelled before any output is produced, and many other projects continue indefinitely without producing results. These projects consume money and resources that could have been used elsewhere. Hence the firm's future depends on that proportion of projects that produce timely, good quality results (see Fig. 1.3). A small reduction in the proportion of money and resources wasted on projects that do not help the business has a disproportionately large benefit for the future of the firm. This is why some firms have realized that project management can be a powerful competitive weapon.

▶ Identifying projects

It is essential that firms identify project-like initiatives so that they can be properly managed. This way, those which require extra effort can be allocated extra resources. Similarly, those that would use up more valuable resources than can be justified by their business benefits should not be pursued. But projects do not always arrive ready defined, with a clear label attached bearing the words 'This is a project'. We have already seen that there is a continuum between slightly unusual day-to-day tasks and small projects. It is quite common for initiatives that are really projects to seem like a slight variation on what is known. If this is the case, then people sometimes only realize that an initiative should have had more management after it has descended into chaos.

So identifying projects is an important skill for any business manager, even if they do not themselves go on to manage the project.

Projects have some or all of the following characteristics:

◆ Projects involve change: this could be as simple as upgrading a single piece of IT hardware, or as complex as integrating the hardware, systems, people and cultures of two companies. This change is what creates value for the firm.

◆ Projects have an objective or end point. Unlike day-to-day activities, which are repeated as required, once a project reaches its objective, it finishes.

◆ Whereas existing, stable business processes provide a known means to get things done, projects often have to tackle problems for which even the method to be used is not clear at the outset. As well as achieving their main objective, these projects must invent their own processes at the same time. Hence projects are more risky than day-to-day business processes.

Other definitions can be used to help project identification. The International Standards Organization defines a project as:

> 'A set of co-ordinated activities, with a specific start and finish, pursuing a specific goal with constraints on time, cost and resources.' (ISO 8402)

This definition extends the set of identifiable characteristics of a project to include constraints on time, cost and resources. Clearly, if we have unlimited time, cost and resources then there is little need for proper management. Reality is such that these things are heavily constrained in any organization subject to competitive pressure (even public sector organizations compete for money and resources) and so projects must be managed.

The widely accepted PRINCE methodology defines a project as:

> 'A management environment that is created for the purpose of delivering one or more business products according to a specified business case.'

Organizations quickly realize that these general definitions must be adapted to their specific circumstances before they can be usefully applied. Common sense suggests that it is necessary to have a lower threshold on the size of activities that are treated as projects, to stop the system becoming overloaded. Many companies adopt guidelines based on expenditure or the number of man-days of effort. For example, in one firm any piece of work involving more than five man-days of effort is treated as a project, whereas in another much larger firm the threshold is set at a total expenditure of £100,000. Your organization may have its own guidelines, but in all cases the point is not the detail of threshold but the intention that projects should be properly managed. Be aware that tasks sometimes start as incidental activities that do not merit all the procedures of a project, and they can then grow and begin to take up more and more effort. If a task is small today but is likely to grow, or it has already started to clash with other projects over resources, then it should be logged as a project even if it does not currently meet all of the criteria. Do not be tempted to adjust your project so that it avoids the company threshold in the hope of avoiding paperwork and delay. Doing so has several consequences:

◆ It uses limited resources on a project which has not been assessed against other potential projects for its value to the organization as a whole. It therefore may be a misuse of company resources.

◆ It is likely to run into difficulty over staff availability since key people will be booked by other projects that have a legitimate claim over them.

◆ It will have substantially higher risk than other projects, since such 'underground' projects are unlikely to use the basic structuring, reviews and supervision processes that keep other projects on track.

▶ Managing projects

If you are contemplating managing your first project, you first need to know that project management is not a zero-time task. It takes effort and energy and time. All of this should be repaid in wastage avoided during the project, but you need to be sure that you can commit the time needed for the management task. If you try to squeeze in your project management responsibilities around other priority activities without doing something to free up the necessary time, then you will almost certainly encounter problems. This is not to say that one can never manage a project at the same time as other activities – it simply means that if your diary is already full, you need to make some space in it before you take on something else. Low-intensity projects that are repeats of projects that the team has done before usually require little supervision, and it is possible to manage several of these at once or manage one such project alongside other day-to-day responsibilities. Projects with larger teams working intensively in new areas require constant management attention, and they need a dedicated full-time project manager. The largest projects can require several full-time project managers – one for each sub-project and one to co-ordinate the others.

Managing projects is unlike managing other activities. Even experienced department managers have to learn new skills if they are to be successful when running projects. Normal ('run the firm') processes either continue indefinitely or reach an end point but are then repeated in an identical form. In either case, this means that the process is well understood by all involved and so the risks are low. Projects are not like this: they have an end point after which the project ceases to exist and team members move on to other tasks. So each project is to some extent unique and the team has to solve unfamiliar problems. Hence, projects usually involve some uncertainty over how the objective will be achieved, and there may even be uncertainty at the outset over whether the objective is achievable. So project risks are far higher than those of normal processes.

Experience shows that these risks can be managed by applying a common set of techniques – project management – that guide the structuring and execution of projects.

A key point in this different approach is that it is driven by risk. Risk is just one of the domains which require constant explicit attention through the life of a project, to a much greater extent than when managing a stable process. These 'Project Management Processes' include the following.

Risk management

A project is subject to more risk than a continuously-running business process, and it is often the case that the more valuable the objective, the higher the risk. However, experience shows that risk can be managed, and projects can succeed despite numerous potential pitfalls if the right techniques are used.

Scope management

One risk is so important that it is treated as a separate area of project management: the risk that the project objectives might change. Nobody would dream of changing the terms of reference of a business unit without considering the consequences, but in projects, it is surprisingly difficult to spot that the terms of reference have changed, and to respond appropriately to that change.

Monitoring and control

The time, resources and money set aside to carry out a project are finite, and the number of tasks to be done is large at the outset, and can get larger as the project unfolds unless there is active monitoring and control. Project managers need some tools to help them understand the true status of the project (how far there really is to go), and also to help them focus their attention on the most critical areas.

Planning

Planning lies at the heart of project management, and yet the standard tools of project planning are often unknown outside the field. Anyone contemplating taking on project management should have a sound grasp of the techniques for project planning.

Everyday basics and administration

The day-to-day tasks of project management involve administration tasks such as running meetings and keeping records. Doing these things properly minimizes the time that must be set aside for them and reduces the potential for further wasted time through misunderstandings.

Organization and team

Projects entail setting up the team that will do the work, and it is important that the right people are available at the right time. Furthermore, there will be new people who must be involved and whose support is essential on each new project, and so the project interfaces are as important as they are between business departments – but they have less time to mature.

▶ Project life cycle outline

Underpinning much of project management is an approach to breaking down the work into self-contained chunks that can be more easily managed. This applies with the delegation of tasks to individuals, and also, at a higher level, to the structure of the whole project. In fact, it is possible to work with a basic structure that applies to the majority of projects, irrespective of the area of application. This is because all projects have to go through the same basic steps: first, we must decide what needs to be done, then we must create the solution, and then we must roll out or implement the solution. In between each of these steps there is usually a management decision to continue with the project. In this book we will use a generic model of a project called the project life cycle to represent this standard way that projects are structured. The project life cycle breaks the work down into phases that correspond to the progress of a general project, and we assume that the management decisions to commit resources coincide with the beginnings of each progress step. This is usually the case, but sometimes the big project decisions occur part-way through one of the development blocks. If this happens then it is important for the good governance of the project that there is a break at the decision point, even though this may mean splitting one of the technical progress steps.

Many organizations have their own models and terminology. The one presented here is typical and covers the necessary ground, but it is likely to differ slightly from what your organization uses. If you find that this is the case then common sense should allow you to resolve inconsistencies – it is almost certain that your organization's model is trying to do the same thing as the framework presented here. On your project, you may believe that one or more of these generic phases is inappropriate for your needs. It is possible that yours is one of those rare projects that really does not need one of the steps – if so, then cut it out. But it is more likely that your project is in an area that uses different terminology to that used here, and what seems irrelevant will be seen to be essential once you translate the words into your usual specialist language. The underlying steps are usually necessary, even if the words are different.

The project life cycle starts when a need for a project is identified. The broad steps are outlined in Fig. 1.4, and each step is explored in more detail later in this book.

Fig. 1.4 Generic project life cycle

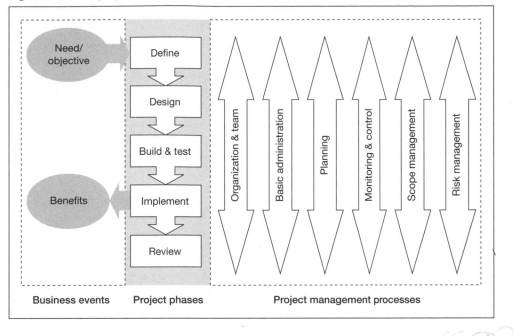

▶ Define

Once a broad need has been identified, the project must be defined. This does not mean that work on creating the desired outputs starts immediately: definition involves clarifying the objectives and what will be involved in achieving them. This involves creating a well-documented description of end-user requirements and deriving a full project plan including timing, resources and costs. It is only once this information is available at the end of the definition phase that a proper decision about whether to proceed with the project can be made. In order to allow such a decision to reflect all relevant facts, the project plan should also include risk management and contingency aspects.

At the end of this phase the various important pieces of information are likely to exist in a variety of formats in different documents. Because organizations need to be able to compare proposed projects on a consistent basis it is normal to summarize this information in a standardized format. We will call this document the Project Initiation Document (PID). Company management will decide whether or not to proceed with a project on the basis of the information in the PID. Acceptance of the project defined in the PID should also mean that the money and resources that it specifies will be made available.

On large projects there may be months or even years of effort involved in planning. This requires the firm to commit significant resources to the planning phase, even if the subsequent project is not pursued. In this case it is normal to carry out a preliminary study to determine whether it is even worthwhile investing the effort to produce a full plan. This preliminary study results in a project proposal that contains broad estimates of the costs and timing of the overall project and a detailed plan for the main project definition phase. Hence on large projects, the define phase can be split into a propose phase and a define phase.

▶ Design

If the project is authorized, then work on creating the desired project outputs can begin. On non-technical projects this may mean data gathering and defining new services or processes. On technical projects work starts with high-level system design, before proceeding to detailed design and development of individual pieces of technology.

▶ Build and test

Once the design of the project output is decided, then it should be possible to build one or more examples of the design and test them to ensure that what has been designed meets the user requirements. Typically, this phase of the project will involve a structured programme of building and testing progressively larger sections of the project output, until the whole set of deliverables is available and validated. Non-technical and software projects may have very few build activities but it is usually necessary to test ideas, methods, products and processes before applying them.

▶ Implement

Even though project outputs might have been shown to meet the requirements originally defined, they only add value to the organization once they have been deployed or adopted. Implementation must be carefully planned and executed to minimize disruption and maximize benefits.

▶ Review

One of the most important ways leading organizations set themselves apart from the rest is that they learn from their experiences: they systematize success and avoid repeating mistakes. Most projects can teach us something, and a brief review after the project has finished has value for the organization.

Ten key questions: before you start

1 Is the need for this project understood and agreed by everyone who will have to contribute resources to it?   Yes/No

2 Do you understand the project authorization and monitoring procedures in your firm?   Yes/No

3 If you take on the management of the project, will you be given the authority to make decisions about the project direction?   Yes/No

4 If this is your first project, will you get support and guidance from more experienced project managers?   Yes/No

5 Do you know why you have been chosen to manage this project? Have you thought through what this tells you about the motivations of the other people involved?   Yes/No

6 Can you commit the time needed to manage this project?   Yes/No

7 Will you be responsible for the initial definition of scope, timing and cost? If these have already been set, can you review and renegotiate them if required?   Yes/No

8 Has the person who had the idea for the project described the concept to you directly in their own words?   Yes/No

9 Do you know enough about your organization's track record with projects? (Which succeeded, which did not, and why?) Have you got the maximum learning from others' experience?   Yes/No

10 Have you read and understood this book? Are you ready, willing and able to apply its lessons?   Yes/No

2
basic principles

Business principles

Management and control principles

People principles

1
2
3
4
5
6
7
8
9
10
11

There are some basic principles that should guide our behaviour throughout any project. If team members, project managers, business managers and everyone else in the firm can rely on these principles always being observed, then many of the common project pitfalls will be avoided. They are grouped here under Business Principles, Management and Control Principles, and People Principles.

▶ Business principles

▶ Projects support the business

A project may have many merits, but it is a basic principle that those which are most closely aligned with the business strategy should receive the greatest support.

Anyone in the organization can have a good idea for a project. This is how we make sure that the projects proposed are addressing real problems, and have the support of an enthusiastic champion. However, the corollary of the fact that someone's unique perspective allows them to see a need for a particular project is that they may not see the perspectives of the organization as a whole. In an ideal world, the organization would provide funding and resources for all the good ideas, but in a world of constrained funding and resources we must be careful about which of the good ideas is pursued. The only rational criterion for such a choice is the way in which the project supports the business.

Most businesses have some sort of strategic plan, but it would be inappropriate to try to have exactly one project which addressed each point of that plan. This is much too simplistic, and would not allow for the rapid responsiveness for which projects are so useful. Nonetheless, it is helpful to think how each proposed project is aligned with strategic objectives. An otherwise excellent idea may just be inappropriate for the direction the organization wants to take.

Projects should also be able to trace their business benefits to improvements in revenues, cost or business risk. If there is no impact on these – even in the medium or long term – then the project is probably an interesting exercise but cannot justify an investment.

▶ Plan the work

Projects must be broken down into tasks that can be individually delegated and managed.

Many studies show that of the time spent on a project, it is that spent on structuring and planning that has the greatest influence on later project success. Projects are too complex for any human being to be successful without using a minimum of structure to get agreement on what is required at the outset, and then provide a map for how to get to the objective. Once the project manager has stood on a high hilltop, so to speak, and drawn the overall map, it is safe for us to venture into the undergrowth, where the occasional glimpse of a landmark is enough for us to know where we are and where to turn. Were we to set off into the undergrowth without the map, or if we chose not to use it, we should expect to get lost.

As well as being necessary for smooth project operations, the plan is the best source of information about the resources and investment needed to deliver a project, and so it is what the firm uses in its decisions about which projects to pursue. The firm needs good plans so that it can select those projects that have the highest ratio of benefits to investment within its strategy and the constraints of the current economic situation.

Plans do not need to be exhaustive in every detail from the first day. They do need to have enough detail for everyone on the project to know what their own tasks are, who depends on their output, when they are on the critical chain, and how their task fits within the larger context of the project.

▶ Manage risk actively

Risks must be identified before they turn into crises, and the plan modified to minimize their likelihood and/or impact, although only in those cases where the business consequences justify such action. Part of risk management is using project structure to prevent tasks from interfering with each other, and including reviews to get periodic independent reconfirmation of project viability.

If we accept that projects involve doing something new, then we must acknowledge that all projects have risks. Risks might originate from various sources, for example:

◆ Application of a technology in a new domain.

◆ Business support for the project and interest in its outputs.

◆ Project size and complexity, requiring ever greater co-ordination.

◆ True market demand for the proposed product.

◆ Market or regulatory changes during the course of work.

Some of these risks are internal to the project, and some external, but to the extent that the project manager is responsible for delivering a set of business benefits, the project manager should have a response ready for all of them. This may seem harsh in the case of risks which are external, but the project manager can always gather information about such risks and can often steer the project around them if they are sufficiently threatening.

In general we do not have to resign ourselves to accepting all risks. Some can be avoided and others minimized. This process is covered in more depth later in this book, but we list the principal points here:

◆ Risks must be identified. This requires that people feel sufficiently comfortable to talk about what they think might go wrong and for them to believe that they will be listened to. So the project manager's tone in looking for risks is crucial for the quality of the list.

◆ Once identified, risks must be ranked or prioritized according to their severity.

◆ The ranked list of risks gives a clear indication of the threats to the project, from the critical high probability/high impact risks that must be addressed, to the low probability/low impact risks that can be ignored.

◆ Each risk can be managed either by:
  – prevention (taking action to prevent the event arising);
  – reduction (taking action to reduce the likelihood and/or the severity of the risk);
  – transference (putting measures in place so that the risk falls outside the project);
  – contingency (putting in place plans which are only enacted if the risk occurs);
  – acceptance (a decision to live with the risk as it is without further action).

◆ The decision over what action to take over a particular risk will depend on the relative balance of the business severity of the risk and the business cost of the management action.

◆ Risk management is not a single exercise done during the planning phase and then forgotten. If it is to be useful in managing a project then it should be repeated and updated as new information becomes available.

Hence good risk management depends on the other basic principles of good communication and good structuring and planning.

▶ Management and control principles

▶ Support critical chain management

The critical chain method on which this book is based delivers great benefits for the organization because it both shortens project timelines and reduces the probability of overruns. But these benefits have a cost, and that is that the organization must change some working practices. This requires commitment and management support across the organization.

Many project managers will be familiar with the concept of the project critical path – that sequence of dependent activities that defines the minimum theoretical project duration, and which therefore needs priority management attention. However, the critical path approach does not allow for the fact that project timing is driven as much by the availability of critical resources as it is by task dependency, and it also has a relatively unsophisticated treatment of the inherent uncertainty of task timings. These issues are addressed in the critical chain method (see Appendix A for a more complete description).

The critical chain method relies on several important differences from other techniques. These differences are such that it would be very difficult for an isolated project manager to run a project using the critical chain unless it is widely understood within the organization and the necessary management support is given. If other managers are unwilling to accept that tasks allocated without a fixed deadline have a high priority or if they will not relinquish multitasking, then the firm will not get all the benefits of the critical chain method.

	Classical approach	Critical chain
Task duration shown in plan	Durations that estimator is very confident can be achieved.	Duration thought to be achievable 50% of time.
Allowance for uncertainty in task duration estimates	Padding within task estimates protects tasks individually. May have contingency reserve at project manager's discretion.	Project buffer between end of last scheduled activity and project end date. Buffer sized statistically to protect aggregate project.
Shortest project duration controlled by . . .	Critical path: sequence of tasks that have zero slack between them from beginning to end.	Critical chain: sequence of tasks that has minimum slack without overloading resources.
Project start date	As soon as possible, to maximize time available before deadline.	Count backwards project duration (including buffer) from deadline. Hence may not start immediately.
Delegated tasks should be finished . . .	No later than planned end date (which usually means on planned date or shortly after).	As soon as possible and handed over so that next task can start early.
Multitasking	Acceptable (so all tasks done in parallel progress more slowly).	Not done: finish one task so that others can use your outputs, then move on to another.
Planning to protect against delay	Risk management plan to prevent risks delaying project.	Risk management plan and feed buffers and resource buffers to protect critical chain tasks from variations in input resources and task timing.
Management focus	Critical path – which may change when non-critical activities overrun. Hence whole project must be watched.	Critical chain – which should not change through the project because of the measures taken to protect it.
Monitoring metrics	Progress, projected completion date, earned value, schedule performance index, cost performance index, etc.	Progress and buffer usage.

▶ Work the plan

The plan is the yardstick against which progress will be judged. The plan is there to be used in the day-to-day management of the project. If reality does not match the plan, then the plan must be updated – not abandoned. Updates to the plan which imply that the project will miss its original targets for completion dates or performance mean that the project must be re-approved before proceeding since this new information may change the project's priority for resources and funding.

The process of creating a plan adds value since it forces thinking about what will be involved in the project. However, even this value is destroyed if the plan is not used. A project that is running without reference to the plan soon becomes difficult to manage as it becomes impossible to communicate efficiently or to co-ordinate activities.

In reality, plans cannot be completely rigid. The planner does not have perfect foreknowledge of everything that will happen, and new information may emerge that will mean that the plan has to change. Updating the plan to reflect current information is part of project management, and is the key activity which tells us where the project stands and what has to happen next. Sometimes, the updated plan will show that the total effort required to complete the project is greater than originally thought. Avoid the temptation to ignore or hide such news. It is better to become aware of this truth sooner rather than later, since the project can then be either relaunched with re-confirmed commitment or halted early so that the maximum unused resources and funding is liberated for other uses.

The simplest way for a project manager to ensure that the plan is used is to carry a copy of the current version everywhere they go, so that it can be pulled out and referred to in any conversation.

This process – plan the work and work the plan – is important from the point of view of those within the project, but it becomes critical when viewed in the context of a portfolio of projects. Each project in the portfolio is there because it will achieve some benefit for the business. If a project goes astray, then not only are its benefits lost to the firm, but the benefits of any other projects which depend on it are also lost. Furthermore, because the money has already been spent, the option to invest in some of the other good ideas which were initially rejected in favour of the failed project has also been lost.

▶ Report the truth

Both within the project and when reporting upwards within the firm, it is essential that management has a true picture. Honesty is all the more valuable when it is difficult.

Much of project management is to do with resolving problems. Tasks that are proceeding smoothly do not attract the project manager's attention. Most problems can be dealt with given enough warning – even those which materially affect the scope, cost or timing of the project can be resolved in a controlled way by re-planning and re-authorizing a project if there is time to do so. The project manager can solve problems for team members that they cannot solve themselves by re-allocating tasks or redefining task scope. However, project managers cannot solve problems they don't know about.

One of the most infuriating experiences as a project manager is discovering, one day before an important deadline, that a team member has been struggling with a problem for a week and will not be able to deliver, but the problem could have been solved or the deadline moved if they had reported it a week ago. The project manager is left having to beg forgiveness for missing the deadline and hoping that nobody asks why they were only given a day's warning that the deadline would be missed if the problem had been known for a week. A failure to report a problem until it is too late has removed all of the project manager's room for manoeuvre.

A project manager's best defence against being put in such an unfortunate position is good communication with the team. Insisting on a weekly progress report from everyone can be useful, but it does not substitute for real conversations conducted in an atmosphere of trust, where nuances about emerging issues can be picked up and investigated in more depth. Project managers should make a point of talking to their team regularly, and should also make sure that everyone has a responsibility to come and talk to the project manager as soon as they become aware of problems.

The project manager's reaction when the first project problem is presented will set the expectations of everyone else on the team: a positive attitude, welcoming the information, will mean that you might get to hear about future problems in time to head them off. Losing your temper or attacking the messenger will mean that you will have a few weeks of calm, when there will not seem to be any more problems, but you will then realize that a whole tangled mess of problems has matured into a full-blown project crisis because everyone was too scared to tell you about them.

So it is an important skill to be able to separate the two questions of 'How did we get into this mess?' from 'How do we get out of this mess?'. When a problem is presented, the clear focus must be on how to solve it. Any discussion of how the situation arose must be directed towards ensuring that the same problem does not happen again within the project. General lessons for future projects should be left for the end-of-project review, and general lessons for individuals should also be left until the end of the project, when a balanced view of their contribution to the whole project is available.

Most organizations spread their spending on projects across a portfolio with a range of risks, so that overall risk and return is balanced. Though they would prefer all projects to be successful, they know that some projects will fail. What makes the difference at the firm-wide level is the proportion of projects that fail and whether the failures can be identified early enough to be able to avoid wasting money and resources. So though you might feel uncomfortable if you discover that your project is not viable, you should take reassurance from the fact that most reasonable organizations value accurate and timely information above soothing reassurance.

▶ Manage scope/time/cost tradeoff

Each project must be managed in a way that preserves the appropriate balance between scope (including quality and quantity of deliverables), timescales and costs. These parameters form the core of the Project Definition Document (PDD), and managing them is the core project management task.

Project management is hard. One of the reasons for this is that it involves reconciling constantly conflicting demands to produce the best possible output in the shortest possible time for the least amount of money (see Fig. 2.1). Removing any one of these three fundamental constraints would make project management easy: if there was unlimited budget or it didn't matter whether the output was useful, then it would be much easier to bring a project in on time. Unfortunately, project managers must satisfy all three conditions, but it is very hard to balance all three factors when they are so difficult to compare. Is it worthwhile delaying the project by a week to produce a more polished result? Should we pay the subcontractors extra to complete their task three days early? Striking the wrong balance will throw away some or all of the anticipated business benefits for the project, but how do we strike the right balance?

Fig. 2.1 The performance/time/cost balancing act

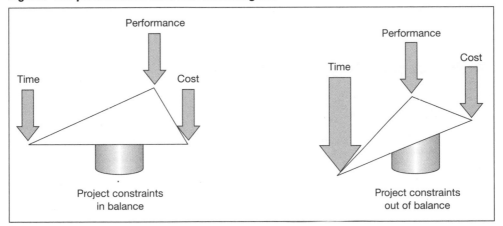

It is in the nature of these conflicting demands that there is no single rule to apply. However, practical guidance is possible:

◆ Use common sense, and never become excessively focused on one of the three conditions to the detriment of the others. It may be that, for example, cash spending is more immediately visible than cutting corners on quality, but common sense says that this is not a good enough reason to shy away from spending some money in order to keep quality adequate.

◆ Make sure that you understand what the business priorities are. If you know that the project must be finished on a particular critical date, then you have a relatively simple criterion for assessing any project decision. Note that there can never be more than one top priority from among these three: if you are told that time *and* scope *and* cost are all the top priority, then you need to continue your enquiries.

◆ If at all possible, find out your business cost of delay – the cost in lost revenues or missed savings of delaying the project output by a day or a week. With this figure in the back of your mind, many of the decisions about how to deal with project events become much easier. However, as with all quick decision aids, be sure that you understand how the figure was generated and what it means in the project context, so that you do not use it inappropriately.

◆ Do not be afraid to refer significant project decisions back to those who originally requested and authorized the project. The user group may not mind reduced functionality at the start, and company management may know that the target date has some flexibility.

◆ Above all, manage scope creep. This is the insidious tendency of projects to pick up additional objectives along the way as work proceeds. Sometimes these additional objectives can be dismissed easily, but some are useful objectives which are done much more efficiently by adding them to the project than by trying to do them separately. Therefore it is important that some suggestions should be accepted and others rejected – and always within the three-way balancing act. This single topic is a common cause of project problems and it is covered in greater depth in a later section of this book.

People principles

▶ Get the right skills

Projects do not always use people from only a single department or group. A project should have access to the skills required, from across the organization.

One of the ways projects add value to organizations is that they are a mechanism to do things which do not fit conveniently into the remit of any single department, and so they allow organizations to do things that would be inefficient within the usual structure.

However, while most people would agree that assembling and using a project team from across the firm is a good thing in principle, it is not always simple to do in practice. The reason for this is that there can be confusion about priorities when people working on the project are answerable both to their line manager and to the project manager. Line managers may agree to make a particular resource available on a certain date, but if the department's priorities change or if the project timescale shifts then the project conflicts with the resource department.

Project managers must be aware that different groups within the firm have their own priorities and sources of information, and good two-way communication is essential. Project managers should:

◆ Make sure that both the line manager and the individual involved are fully aware of the project, its skills requirements, its likely timing, and the work intensity. This should involve regular updates as the project progresses and better information becomes available about the precise timing of a department's involvement.

◆ Get explicit agreement from both the individual and their line manager that, during the time set aside for project work, the project is the priority: there should be no attempt to multi-task or to squeeze in project work around other activities.

They can return to other tasks after, but not during, their project work – the resultant pressure to complete their project work early can help both the project and the line department.

♦ Escalate problems to the project sponsor before they affect the project. The sponsor should be able to help resolve resourcing problems directly, or suggest alternative actions which will protect the project business benefits.

♦ Agree the responsibility for technical supervision and quality control of the work of technical specialists brought into the team. It is entirely possible that a team will include specialists for whom no other team member is qualified to provide technical supervision. In this case, it is usually necessary to involve the individual's line manager in a project supporting role. This can improve communications and understanding between line managers and the project, but if their input is to be worthwhile then the project manager should communicate clearly the scope of each piece of work, and make clear that delegating the technical review role to line managers does not give them the right to change the scope, content or timing of the work package without agreement.

▶ Two-way communication

The ability to communicate effectively is at least as important as technical skill. Communication involves both transmitting a clear succinct message, and making the effort to listen actively.

Project managers are the focal point of communications in the project. Good communication leads to efficient working, good morale and project success – but a project whose manager cannot communicate effectively is doomed to struggle.

Good communication involves more that just speaking and writing: good management involves receiving information at least as much as transmitting. Project managers must build an atmosphere of trust on the project so that people will share information. They must seek out information actively, using questions which do not presuppose the answer. When information is made available the project manager must listen. It is easy to agree with this in principle, but during the hectic lead-up to a project deadline, when communication is most important, it is easy to have a brief conversation without making the effort actually to listen to what is being said. A quick glance at the list of barriers to listening shown in Fig. 2.2 should help to improve reception.

Another temptation when time is short is to eliminate meetings and rely instead on general circulation e-mails. Both meetings and e-mails have a role but they are not interchangeable. One is an opportunity for two-way communication, and the other is deliberately one-way only. Meetings allow rich person-to-person exchange of information, much of which can be of the non-verbal kind that carries significant meaning. An exchange of e-mails may have some of the characteristics of a conversation, but it loses much of the richness of a real conversation (could you pick up the cues from an e-mail which would allow you to ask '. . . OK, but isn't there something else you want to talk to me about?'), and because people delay answering e-mails until they are ready it is sometimes slower.

Fig. 2.2 Barriers to listening

Filtering: listening for something specific but ignoring everything else.

Placating: you agree with everything – but only because you are not really involved.

Dreaming: half-listening until some private association is triggered, then . . . (This is particularly common when anxious or bored.)

Being right: refuse to listen to suggestions, criticism and comments; anything but face the fact that someone might have proved you wrong.

Derailing: changing the subject before they have finished.

Judging: you already know that this person isn't worth listening to.

Mind-reading: second-guessing what they really mean rather than what they are in fact saying.

Sparring: so quick to argue or raise counterpoint that they never *feel* heard. Avoid by replaying what you've just heard.

► Set SMART objectives

ALWAYS set objectives which are:

- ◆ Specific
- ◆ Measurable
- ◆ Achievable
- ◆ Realistic
- ◆ Timed

Objectives are required to give direction and purpose to activities. Having an objective allows individuals some chance of using their initiative in an appropriate way, rather than just doing a task without being able to apply the intelligence to do it better or to adapt to changed circumstances. Everyone knows this, but it is common for objectives to be described imprecisely, with obvious consequences. In the same way that the project as a whole must be defined with identifiable outputs and agreed timing at the outset, individual tasks must be clearly defined.

The 'SMART' acronym helps us to remember the important points when defining work packages.

Specific

What is the exact scope? What is included and what is not? What might be thought to be included but is being done by someone else? What is to be done with the outputs?

Measurable

What measure will we use to know that the task is truly finished? What test must be passed? What format must the output take so that it can be used directly by dependent activities?

Achievable

A delegated impossibility is still impossible! If there is doubt over whether a task is achievable, then the first part of any work package should be either to test feasibility, or to identify what would have to be changed in order to make the rest feasible.

Realistic

What is a realistic task for a sector expert to undertake in a week may not be realistic for a junior joiner in a month. A series of roll-out meetings might be done in two weeks, but clashes with public and personal holidays could mean that a month is required.

One of the tests of a good project plan is that it always deals with the reality of how long it will take to do things, rather than how long we would like it to take if we could ignore inconvenient facts. If the project manager has made an unrealistic plan, it is not acceptable to try to compensate by delegating unrealistic tasks to the team.

Timed

A task without a clear specification of its timing priority is likely to be put to the bottom of the list: it will not get done. The simplest way to make sure that tasks get done is to agree a realistic deadline, even for those tasks which are not time-critical for the project.

This simple approach must be used with care on critical chain projects, because the existence of a distant deadline often actually delays people from starting work. Project managers should still be very clear about the required timing for critical chain tasks: the 'as soon as possible' label on such tasks should be understood to mean exactly what it says.

▶ Responsibility with authority

Once responsibility for a task or a project has been delegated, then the authority to take the decisions needed to get to the agreed objective is also delegated.

The project manager will have neither the time nor the skills to take every decision that needs to be made on a project. Team members have to be trusted to make decisions about how to do things within their own area, otherwise the project manager quickly becomes the project bottleneck. The experience of entrusting the project to someone else can be unsettling for a manager, but it is necessary. There is often a temptation to retain a little control, especially in those cases where the work is in a domain with which the project manager is familiar. Doing so defeats the purpose of delegating: once the team member has the task, they should be allowed to get on with it.

Nonetheless, authority goes hand in hand with responsibility. A team member who agrees to take on a task (remember SMART objectives!) should feel that getting that task done is now their responsibility, and they will be held accountable for the outcome. Taken to its extreme, this might mean that some people's sense of responsibility for their own task leads them to take decisions which damage the project as a whole. In order to guard against this, project managers should not only give autonomy within delegated tasks, but should also specify clearly the boundaries of the responsibility and the associated authority.

A special case of the linkage between authority and responsibility is the project manager role itself. The project manager has the responsibility to deliver the project, and the authority to choose how to do that. However, that authority is conditional on the project running smoothly. If the project looks likely to miss its business objectives, then that authority must be reconfirmed before proceeding.

▶ Team orientation

It is worthwhile investing energy in building team spirit. Managers must manage morale, personality 'fit', and should also encourage team thinking.

No matter how important the project, or how detailed the plan, the project cannot succeed unless people work together effectively. The most successful projects are often those on which the people have started to function as a true team, helping each other, providing energy and cross-fertilization between individuals.

These successful project teams rarely happen by accident. They happen because the right personalities were involved and found good ways to work together. There is no magic formula to ensure that a group of people will gel into an effective team, but it is the project manager who has the most influence in this process. The key points are:

◆ Personalities and working styles matter in a team, and are a valid criterion for team membership selection.

◆ The project manger's level of energy, commitment and enthusiasm will be quickly and intuitively understood by the team members.

◆ The project manager's response to the first project crisis will set how the team deals with inconvenient facts henceforth. An open, positive and solution-seeking attitude to problems will get more problems dealt with while they are small, whereas intimidation and blame will mean that problems get hidden, only to explode later.

◆ Time spent working alongside each other is extremely valuable, and usually makes for much higher technical quality output as well as fostering team spirit.

Part II

project management processes

3

project organization and team

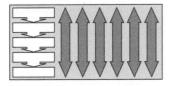

Projects must be broken down into manageable chunks, but the manager's job runs through all the chunks from the beginning of the project to the end. This job has many aspects, and in some ways it parallels the job of a company chief executive: policies must be set, plans made, customers listened to, costs managed, tasks allocated, and finance providers kept informed. All of this must be done not just to get it out of the way, but with a clear direction towards the goal of helping the firm. Project managers are busy people.

In this chapter, we will cover some of these project management tasks in more depth.

What do we mean by project organization and team?

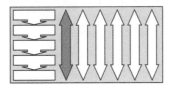

Work does not get done by projects; it gets done by people. Managing projects means managing people. A project manager needs to realize that this means that all those soft people issues that rarely get discussed are going to affect your ability to do your job. Here we present an overview of the topic but it is a topic of such importance that managers of all kinds should take every opportunity to learn more.

Before covering the people issues, it is worthwhile reviewing the various roles that people can play on a project.

Project roles

Though different organizations may have different names for the roles, most will recognize the underlying responsibilities of the roles described here. This split of responsibilities has been found to be the most efficient way for projects to be controlled within an organization where many projects may be under way at once. If yours is the only project in the organization then you may not need some of the roles, but if your organization is trying to run several projects at once without, for example, sponsors or a programme board, then there is likely to be widespread misallocation of money and resources.

▶ Sponsor

The project sponsor is a senior manager who wants the project, usually because it will benefit them in some way. In some cases the sponsor may see the need for the project themselves, but in other cases the suggestion may come from elsewhere in the firm and the sponsor then adopts the idea. If there are several senior managers who will all benefit from the project then it is important that this group agrees to nominate a single representative to avoid confusion.

The sponsor's role is necessary because it is impractical for the whole management of the organization to be involved in every supervision decision. The organization therefore charges the individual who hopes to get the benefits of a successful project with the responsibility and authority for project supervision. This is not the same as project management – it is rather someone who acts as the buyer of the project on behalf of the firm. Conceptually, the sponsor has a business need for the project, the firm grants the sponsor the money and resources for the project, and the sponsor then contracts with the project team to execute the project. Hence in project organization terms the project manager works for the project sponsor, who works for the business.

The sponsor's focus is on the business objectives, and it is common for there to be little contact with the sponsor other than at major project events except if the project is drifting off track and it looks like the business objectives will not be met. It is the sponsor who has the final responsibility to protect the business by intervening if required to get the project back on track or, if necessary, to cancel the project before extra money is wasted.

▶ Project manager

The project manager contracts with the sponsor to manage the project defined in the Project Initiation Document. In most organizations, the project manager has authority to use money and resources up to the limits set out in the PID, but no more. If the project manager learns that the project will take more than was authorized when the PID was approved then it is vital to seek re-approval on the new basis otherwise the project manager will have no authority to proceed.

The project manager plans, organizes, controls and reports project activities. On smaller projects, the project manager may also undertake some of those activities.

▶ Team member

Team members carry out tasks or groups of tasks specified by the project manager, with agreed deliverables and to agreed timescales. Team members are expected to take responsibility for their own tasks, to keep the project manager informed about progress and to exercise initiative if they become aware of other factors outside their specific task that might also affect the project.

▶ Programme board

In most organizations where there are several projects running at once there is a committee that meets regularly to oversee the project portfolio (a programme is a co-ordinated family of projects). The programme board reviews, approves and prioritizes project proposals as well as authorizing resource allocation. It monitors project exceptions and instigates corrective action.

▶ Project support office

Some companies run enough projects to justify having a small department whose role is to support projects and project managers. The details of the role will vary but it may include such things as:

◆ Selecting and supporting project planning software.

◆ Co-ordinating project resource usage across the organization – possibly by maintaining the resource databases linked to the organization's project planning software.

◆ Disseminating best practice in project management across the firm, for example by arranging training or by ensuring that all project managers use the company projects handbook if there is one. The project support office may be a valuable source of advice for people just taking on their first project.

◆ Representing the projects' function in discussions within the firm concerning infrastructure, quality procedures and so on.

◆ Creating and maintaining standard forms for project proposals, PIDs, checklists and commonly-used project procedures.

◆ Possibly, collating project proposals and progress reports on behalf of project managers and handling the interface with the programme board. This may also mean a responsibility for checking and enforcing minimum standards in the documentation submitted.

▶ Stakeholders

Each project will have a group of interested individuals inside and sometimes outside the organization. These may include:

◆ The direct users of the project output.

◆ Those elsewhere in the organization whose day-to-day jobs will be affected by the project.

◆ Managers and team members of other projects which depend on this project to provide either certain outputs or to make resources available by a certain date.

◆ People outside the organization who have a particular view about what the organization or the project are trying to achieve and who may cause considerable damage to the organization's good name if they feel that actions are inappropriate.

◆ Previous buyers of goods or services who may react positively or negatively to news about the development.

◆ Suppliers and distributors who may be fearful that the changes implied by the project will mean a loss of business.

The role of such groups in a project must be dealt with on a case-by-case basis. Projects can have far-reaching effects and one of the potential pitfalls of project management is to believe that the only people who matter are those on the project team and the end-users. Stakeholders is a loose category but the unifying features are that their opinion matters in some way, and they often choose themselves rather than being appointed by the project manager. Their impact can be very great on some projects and in some sectors companies have developed standard contingency plans that are applied on all projects. On the positive side, a network of enthusiastic supporters of a project is one of the hallmarks of a truly successful project and can itself contribute to that success.

Stakeholder management has much in common with public relations, but project leaders do not need to become public relations specialists. On small projects it is usually enough to remember that there are interested parties outside the formal project boundary, and to make an effort to communicate with them.

▶ Specialist advisors

Expert advisors can often add value quickly if they are used appropriately to address a specific problem within their area of expertise. Such inputs from internal or external experts may not merit full inclusion in the project team, though time and budget will always have to be set aside for briefing.

▶ External suppliers

It is common for projects to rely on external suppliers for some of their critical outputs. The supplier might take on a sub-project but you, the project manager, are still responsible for overall delivery and the project manager should manage the supplier with no less care and attention than internal resources. Suppliers should be set SMART objectives and be required to give timely and accurate progress reports like other members of the team.

▶ End-users and end-user representative

The end-users are the people through whom the business benefits of the project will be obtained. They take the project output and use it to improve the organization's performance. This makes them a critically important group.

Their most formal relationship with the project is usually in specifying the user needs at the beginning of the project, and in accepting the project outputs at the end. During the project, the role of the end-users will vary but they will usually be called upon to provide continuing guidance throughout the life of the project in order to ensure that the outputs never diverge from what they should be.

In order to keep communications working effectively it is normal for the user group to appoint a single point of contact to handle the interface with the project. In some cases this representative may need to have the authority to make binding decisions on behalf of the user group, including the decision to accept or reject changes in the project objectives.

eg

Government of Singapore

Public sector bodies do not have a good reputation for project management, and the common problems with IT projects make government IT projects a particularly rich source of disaster stories. But in Singapore, most government IT projects are delivered on time and on budget. This feat arises from the rigorous application of some basic principles along the same lines as those described in this book. For example:

◆ Good project management skills are applied within a recognized framework that allows good project control.

◆ Plans are built around realistic estimates of timings, costs and resource needs.

◆ Every project has a sponsor who is held accountable for project success.

▶ Team management

Technology plays a substantial role in many projects and many project managers and team members have well-developed technology skills. Technology skills are necessary, but are they sufficient? It should be clear by now that project management is not a technology problem. Neither is it a data analysis problem or a market knowledge problem or a sales problem. Instead, it is all about organizing and working with people. Most people have the communications and people skills needed for basic project management, whether they are technologists, analysts, marketers or salesmen. However, some of these skills may need some polishing in order to be of value in project work since there is never time to use trial and error on projects. Even people who are quite good at the people management issues may not know why they do what they do, and so may have difficulty choosing the right course of action in a project that presents new challenges.

▶ Team selection

Every project manager wants the best experts on the team, but what if the best aren't available? And what if the best technical expert is available but only because nobody else will work with them? This is not some fuzzy side issue that you can ignore. Your team have got to be able to work together, and it is part of your job as a project manager to think about this.

Is there such a thing as a perfect team member? We might imagine a genius who knows every corner of their technical field, never gets sick, and always files their documents properly. What would you feel like having to work next to this person? Your answer probably reveals much about the sorts of people you like to work with and so the real answer to the question about the perfect team member is that it depends on who else is in the team. Every project team is different and what is perfect in one will not work in another. So it is neither possible nor desirable to provide precise rules for team selection other than to say that fit with individuals in the team should be a factor.

Within this overall context, there are a few areas to consider:

◆ People like to work with friends, or at least people with whom they have worked in the past. Getting to know new people takes time and intellectual and emotional energy, and most people will save themselves the effort if possible. This means that an entirely new team in which nobody has worked together before will not work at full capacity until some time after the start. Contact time is needed to establish who is who and how people like to work together. If your project team is widely dispersed then they will probably never really understand how each project member works unless you make a special effort to bring them together to work as a group at the start of the project. If the activities in your plan are well compartmentalized and you have briefed everyone well, then it is possible to run the project without the team knowing each other. But this is rarely beneficial.

◆ If a team is made up mostly of people who have worked together before, with one or two new faces, then take care to ensure that the new joiners fit. Groups develop their own subculture and a new joiner can sometimes break the rules without noticing; this can sometimes lead to rejection of the new joiner unless someone realizes what is going on and intervenes. This theory is easy but these situations are hard to spot. The rejection will be a matter of subtle group dynamics and it may not be obvious that it has happened. A new joiner may feel isolated and demotivated when it becomes obvious that everyone on the team is friendly with everyone else except them. The rest of the team in this situation is being lazy about including the joiner, but people cannot be ordered to be friendly. Take special care to emphasize that the joiner belongs to the group and to ensure that they do not get left out of group social activities. There is a particular version of this problem if you, the project leader, are the new person on an existing team. This is examined in more depth below.

◆ Teams under pressure tend to reach for and adapt the first likely-looking solution. If a team has worked together on a similar problem before, they are very likely to revert to their previous solution if they need to save time. This reuse of pre-existing solutions is an excellent example of organizational learning and is one of the ways that firms build competitive advantage. However, not every problem is amenable to the same solution, and every framework only has a limited lifespan before a fundamentally new approach must be found. If a creative solution is needed, then a fresh team is almost certainly needed, with as much diversity as possible. Diverse groups of individuals may go through an uncomfortable phase as they struggle to find ways to work together, but this is also the way to make sure that we consider the widest possible spectrum of approaches before settling on a solution. So think about your need for creativity and choose your team accordingly.

◆ Not every project team that has worked together before wants to work together again. If the earlier project has strained relationships then you may be better off not burdening your project with this emotional legacy. Don't assume that all previous experience is positive.

▶ Gaining and maintaining authority

One of the stressful parts of becoming a project manager is often the idea that you will somehow have to establish authority over people who have hitherto been your peers. 'Won't it be obvious that I know less than everyone else about most of the aspects of the work? Won't they see through me?' Many successful project managers admit that they started with just the same fears. It did not stop them doing a good job.

The good news is that most people will be on your side. Your team want you to succeed because that means project success, which is good for them as well. Most people do not expect you to be an expert in their domain as well as yours – after all they would probably not have been brought into the team unless they had some specialist skills. Furthermore, the firm also wants you to succeed and will give support and guidance if you ask for it. Your position as a manager gives you a natural source of authority. The simple fact that you are the manager predisposes people to fulfil your requests – you have the weight of convention and organizational protocol behind you. Even friends can usually respond appropriately and professionally when you move into the project manager role as long as you do not give out mixed signals when in the professional setting.

The authority that comes from your position as project manager is called legitimate power. There are other sources of power that you may also have:

◆ **Reward power:** the capacity to grant a reward that someone wants.

◆ **Expert power:** specialist knowledge that means your opinion carries weight. The importance of expert power varies, but it is hard to get taken seriously in some technical domains without some technical knowledge, and in extreme cases members of some professions refuse to be managed by anyone who is not themselves a member.

◆ **Referent power:** the power of your personal network. If you are the son or daughter of the chief executive you have considerable power in the organization even though you may hold a junior post. By all means use your network to help your project but beware of using this power in ways that harm others or allow you to short-cut the normal channels. You do not want to acquire the reputation that goes with excessive use of referent power.

◆ **Coercive power:** in some ways the reverse of reward power – it is the capacity to inflict some unwanted outcome on someone who does not do as you wish. Any use of coercive power is likely to destroy whatever enthusiasm an individual may have had, even if it produces the desired action in the short term.

You can either build on your initial advantages, or destroy them. Common sense usually makes the difference between these two outcomes.

Do	Don't
◆ Treat everyone as adults. Tell them what needs to be done and why, and let them get on with it.	◆ Take credit for anyone else's work.
◆ Ask for people's opinions about their area and listen to the answer.	◆ Give the impression that you don't trust people by not accepting the professional opinion of people who know more about the area than you.
◆ Praise good work publicly.	◆ Attack or insult anyone on the team, even if you feel angry about something.
◆ Share information about things within and beyond the project.	◆ Attempt to win favour with the team by breaking confidences with others in the firm. (Can the team then trust you?)
◆ Remember that making people ask for your signature or give you an account of how they spent their time reminds them who is boss.	◆ Bark orders like a drill sergeant. If you let your fear drive you to this, people might even not take you seriously.
◆ Ask people to do things in just the same way you would normally – politely and professionally.	◆ Refuse to get involved with group social activities – you will be seen as aloof.
◆ Refer to and be seen with the senior people with whom you have to deal.	◆ Shoot the messenger.
◆ Respond to bad news by looking for a solution, not a culprit.	◆ Use coercive power (not even if they deserve it).

These dos and don'ts are pretty much the same as they would be for any group management function. What is different in project management is that you might have to become very skilled at these basics because new projects, with new teams, will come along far more frequently than they would if you were in a line management position.

Another way that project management differs from line management is that project management involves more uncertainty about what to do and how to do it. Projects, by their nature, involve doing things in new ways and some part of the work is likely to go beyond established procedure. The team looks to the project manager to give guidance and set direction under these circumstances, and if they get the impression that you are vague and confused, you will begin to lose credibility. But be wary of being decisive merely for appearance's sake since this can be equally damaging to your credibility. Your best defence against this is the project plan. If you have thought through all the issues, considered all the possible approaches and planned the project in a way that gives the best balance of risks and progress, then you will already know most of the answers. Refer back to the plan, remind yourself why it was set up this way, and give a clear answer. Project managers who try to work without making or referring to a plan lose credibility with their teams not because the teams pay direct attention to the plan itself, but because the manager appears indecisive and keeps contradicting earlier decisions.

> ## Common sense
>
> Everybody makes mistakes – even you. Sometimes you can recover the situation before anyone notices, but sometimes somebody will realize that they are having to work harder because of a mistake you made. Some people never ever admit that something was their fault, even if it is obvious, and some go so far as to intimidate anyone who dares to point it out or to suggest another way that is clearly better. If you behave this way you will achieve two things: you will eventually erode the morale of your team, starting with the most intelligent, and you will ensure that no ideas other than your own get implemented. Since nobody can challenge these ideas of yours the bad ones will not be filtered out, and your project will suffer.
>
> If you suspect that this description might apply to you – or more importantly, that your team believes that it applies to you, it is in your interests to change your behaviour. The change is easy: all you have to do is to admit that you are wrong once in a while. Try it. You will find that instead of losing respect you gain it, by showing that you are mature enough to take responsibility for your own actions. This does not mean you have to fawn constantly, just that you should not hide behind your managerial power. If you have made a mistake you might even find it easier to get people to help you out by apologizing and asking for their support than by announcing the extra workload and leaving them to deduce the reasons themselves.

▶ Work styles

Isn't it amazing that some people get any work done at all, considering how much time they spend chatting? If you know someone who is like that, ask yourself whether they have ever produced answers to questions faster than you could have done, just by knowing who to ask instead of trying to generate the answer themselves. If, instead, you are yourself someone who always finds the answer through your network, maybe you secretly admire or despise those people who try to work everything out for themselves instead of making use of perfectly good pre-existing information. The point of all this is that different people have different operating styles (see Fig. 3.1). You are much more likely to have to deal with different styles in cross-functional project management than if you stay within your own domain as different domains attract different sorts of people.

There are many theories about personalities and people's preferred team roles but it is sufficient here to point out that these differences are real and can bring down the unwary project manager. Do not assume that everyone works in the same way that you do, and manage the working styles in your team actively. That means choosing the right mix of people and adapting your own style to suit circumstances.

One way to think of the working style problem is that there are two ways people can spend work time together: they can either be businesslike, with a focus on getting the job done ('task oriented'), or they can focus on the person in front of them and deal with the human issues ('maintenance oriented'). In the course of a normal day, or even a single conversation, most people spend part of their time in task and part in maintenance. Maintenance time is the glue that holds groups of people together as a coherent group. By investing time and energy in authentic conversations that touch areas of life outside the immediate task, the bonds that tie the group together are maintained. So as a project manager with a newly formed group, you should expect to have to invest time and energy (maybe even deliberately chosen time outside work hours, as a signal of your commitment to the human side) to get the team together. Once people feel good spending time together it becomes easier for them to talk about task problems and interact effectively without worrying too much about what other people think. Suggestions for improvements are easier to make to friends than to strangers. Some maintenance time after a gruelling period in the run-up to a project deadline is well spent, and will keep the team working for the rest of the project.

Everyone has a natural predisposition towards either task or maintenance activities. In extreme examples, some people are so wrapped up in their work that they don't seem to notice anyone else around them, and others are so warm and chatty that they really do get nothing done. Teams made up of a range of people work best if there is a balanced range of predispositions, and everybody can do a bit of both. When you are thinking about the balance in your team do not be afraid to bring in someone you know is maintenance oriented if it will bring balance to a team of task-focused people. A single task-focused person can do much to bring closure and get some momentum going in a group of otherwise maintenance-oriented people.

Fig. 3.1 Personal styles

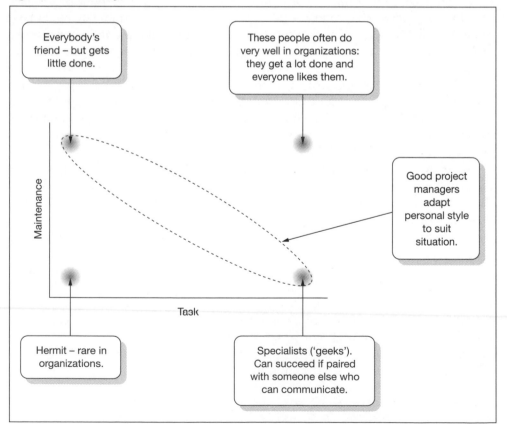

As project manager, your special responsibility is to fill the gaps between the working styles of the team members and adapt your style to match circumstances. When the deadline is looming, you must have built up enough of a reserve of good-will through your previous behaviour that you can behave in a directive manner, giving orders with little explanation if necessary. Judge when it is safe to have some fun together and when the team has really got to get down to some hard work, then set an appropriate example.

> **!**

Common sense

It is good for team spirit to spend time together socializing. Knowing this, the obvious thing to do is to go out for a drink together after work. This is just what friends do together, and everyone will work better together as a result. But don't expect it to be good for everyone. Some people just don't like it: maybe they have family commitments, or they just don't enjoy going to the sorts of places that you enjoy. Sometimes pressing everyone to come along may be counterproductive: nobody can be ordered to have fun. If there are people who are clearly uncomfortable with the suggested outing, it is pointless to insist. Next time, choose a different time or event, and if you must, just make sure that these people get included in group events during work hours.

▶ Morale

People do good work because they want to. It might give them a sense of achievement directly or they might feel good about doing their bit for the team. People will go to great lengths if positively motivated but if demotivation sets in, your project could be in serious trouble. If you have ever felt demotivated yourself, you will know that deadlines just don't seem to matter and benefits lost to the firm aren't even worth a shrug. Only a personal appeal from a friend can get you to do anything when you feel like this, and this is one of the key issues with motivation: it usually has little to do with threats and rewards, and lots to do with relationships. Threatening or coercing someone can only ever get compliance, not enthusiasm, and will make future motivation harder because relationships will be harmed. Even offering rewards does not always help. Rewards can get people to change their behaviour if they care about the reward, but this also means that people concentrate more on ticking all the boxes they need to claim the reward rather than on delivering the underlying product or service.

Experience shows that the things that build motivation are different from the things that can destroy it. Top of the list of factors that build motivation are a sense of achievement, recognition, work that is in itself satisfying, a sense of responsibility, and the chance of advancement. Top of the factors that destroy motivation are irrational policies and administrative procedures, and excessively close supervision that implies a lack of trust.

So the best way of managing motivation is by using the same basic personal communication tools you use for everything else.

◆ Build your relationship with the person as well as the job function.

◆ Use common sense when deciding the necessary level of project documentation, and make sure that everyone understands why this is necessary.

◆ Let people know that you notice good work and extra effort.

◆ Make sure that people understand why their task is important.

◆ Show that you trust and rely on the person.

◆ Protect team members from demoralizing uncertainty over the project direction or justification.

> **!**

> ### Common sense
>
> Both enthusiasm and despair are infectious. A radiantly enthusiastic project manager can energize the team, making everybody's tasks seem easier and more enjoyable. But if you are despairing be aware that the team will be guided by your attitude. This does not mean that you should ever conceal what is happening: it is essential that everyone on the team understands the facts of the situation so that their own project decisions reflect reality. But it does mean that despondency on your part will be amplified through the team, and will make problems worse.

▶ Supervision

The project manager's responsibility to maintain the balance of the time/cost/performance tradeoff means that project activities must be supervised. You need to know that the deliverables are on track, and you need to intervene if you believe that there is a problem. This amounts to little more than a re-statement of the project manager job title, so why spend time on it here? As is often the case, the principle is easy, but the practical implementation needs care.

Most project managers develop a personal system for supervising activities. Some take a formal approach with a lot of scheduled reporting and others practise what is called 'management by walking around' – that is, just making a tour of the desks of the project team, chatting about whatever they are doing, and following your instinct about who to talk to next. Either approach is potentially viable, but each can be dangerous if they are applied without being adapted to suit individual team members. Some people need more supervision than others, and applying the same process to everyone risks annoying the senior people while leaving the junior people feeling adrift and unsure that their work is useful.

Sometimes, you may have to deal with someone who thinks that they know everything, but whose attitude in fact reveals that they do not even know how much else there is to learn. In these circumstances careful supervision is required to cover the technical gaps but this individual probably believes that supervision is not needed. Some lateral thinking can help: use the project plan to insert some extra formal quality assurance checks in a way that is less personally threatening than constantly checking up on progress. At the same time, try to pair the individual with a more senior team member so that they can share tasks. This way, day-to-day supervision is delegated.

It is a basic instinct to want to check up on everything as a deadline approaches, just to make sure that it is all going to be alright. This is an excellent habit for a project manager to get into. But don't take it too far. There comes a point when everyone knows what has got to be done, all the inputs are available, and all that remains is to do the work; going round and checking again actually slows things down. The best thing you can do at this stage is simply to clear all the minor obstacles out of the way of the people who will do the work, and let them get on with it. If the person responsible for the last-but-one critical chain activity has to leave the office to get their car serviced, then your best action is not to check their work again, but to offer to take care of the car while they stay and get on with the work!

> ## ! Common sense
>
> One of the reasons that project management can be stressful is the uncomfortable feeling that you will be held responsible for other people's mistakes. You are the manager and you are responsible for delivering the project, and the buck stops with you. If someone on your team lets you down then it is still your problem, even though you did everything possible to help that person succeed. A project manager who publicly blames a team member for the delay in delivery looks foolish, so you end up taking the blame yourself.
>
> To some extent, this tension is a fact of life for any manager and you will have to live with it. But do not ruin your life by letting yourself feel responsible for every mistake that happens. If you have really delegated responsibility and authority together, then the person to whom the task was delegated must accept responsibility for the task outcome. If you suspect that an individual has not fully understood that their actions have a direct impact on the customer, then let the person talk to the customer directly and experience the reaction at first hand. In the same way that a good project manager should never take the credit for somebody else's good work, you should find a way to allow team members to feel the negative consequences of their actions as well.

everyday basics and administration

1
2
3
4
5
6
7
8
9
10
11

What do we mean by everyday basics and administration?

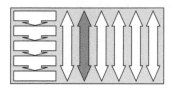 One view of the project manager's job is that it is not to *do* project work, but to clear the obstacles out of the way that would prevent the other team members from doing project work. This is perhaps extreme, but it illustrates a point. Everyone has had the frustrating experience of trying to get a morning's work done only to find that it is already lunch-time and all you have done is look for a document that was filed in the wrong place, and then deal with a stream of queries on things that you thought were finished long ago. It is part of a project manager's job to try to run the project in such a way that team members have the minimum of time wasted in this way.

Time recording

▶ Rationale

Organizations set aside a certain proportion of their staff to work on projects. These people cost money, both in direct employment costs and in indirect overhead costs. Organizations therefore need to ensure that the benefits they obtain from projects outweigh the costs of the people involved, but this is very hard to do if there is no way to know how people are actually spending their time. Using the time requirements information from the project plan is a good first step. However, projects can overrun and tasks can be re-allocated, and it is under these circumstances that the best information is needed.

Within a project, it is also useful to know where all the time is going.

▶ Process

For the firm as a whole, it is usually sufficient to know how many days each week a person has spent on each project. Within the project, it can be useful to break this down to individual tasks so that we can track progress against tasks.

The most appropriate way to do this may vary with project circumstances and the management information systems available. If the project is forced to operate without any other time-recording tools, then a spreadsheet completed weekly by all team members should be used. This serves two purposes: it builds up a record of what time has actually been spent on the project, and it provides an opportunity for the project manager to gather the more project-critical data on how much work there is still to do. Knowing that four days of effort were spent on a task this week is interesting, but it is much more interesting for the project manager to know whether the end of the task is four days closer than it was a week ago, or whether it is five days closer (we have made good progress) or three days closer (we have encountered obstacles). Hence, any tool you use for time recording should provide a means for people to give a new estimate of remaining work.

Depending on the IT tools used, some or all of this can sometimes be done online on the company intranet. Project planning software, accounts systems and time reporting systems can sometimes be integrated so that an individual's time reports roll through automatically into an updated project plan, with updated costs and projected completion. This improves the quality and the immediacy of the information available to the project manager and to the firm, while eliminating manual rekeying of data. If it is available, such a system should be used.

▶ Meetings

▶ Rationale

Does anyone need any explanation about how to make meetings useful? Isn't it something that everyone should have picked up automatically early in their career? Of course, everyone has attended meetings that did not seem to achieve much, and everyone knows somebody who, even after decades in the business, does not seem to be able to run a meeting. This may not be a serious barrier in some jobs, but it matters more for project managers. Project managers spend more of their time in meetings, whether formal or informal, than other members of the project team, and so poor meetings skills are more costly for the project manager. Furthermore, meetings are usually the forum where the most valuable information is exchanged between different groups, and decisions are taken that affect the whole project. So the difference between a good and a bad meeting can have an impact on the project out of all proportion to the time involved.

▶ Process

The key to a successful meeting is preparation. Quick impromptu discussions require less preparation than formal presentations, but some preparation is always required. The most basic requirements are to be absolutely clear in your own mind what the issue is, and what you want to achieve by the meeting. What is the one question to which we need an answer? With a good understanding of the issue, it becomes much easier to know what sort of meeting is required. Is it a question that could be answered by one of the project team alone from immediately available information? If so, go and ask the question at your team member's desk. Does it involve sharing information between different groups before a group decision can be made? If so, think through who has to be involved and set up a more formal meeting. If you cannot identify the basic issue, then do not take up other people's time trying to find an answer to a problem you cannot pose coherently. Instead, consider holding a different meeting with a more limited agenda and attendance, simply to identify what the issue really is. A quick preliminary discussion with one or two other people can bring clarity to the agenda of a larger meeting without trying to solve the problem identified.

Identifying the core issue should allow you to plan the meeting:

- Who needs to be present at the meeting?
- What information do they hold that other people will need?
- Who needs to be present for reasons of communication or simply to witness that the decision was made rationally?
- Do we have people with the authority to take the decisions we know will need to be made? (If the right person is simply not available in time, do not just go ahead regardless: try to get the authority holder to send a named delegate who is given the authority to take the necessary decision in this meeting. Otherwise you may end up having a meeting without any useful outcome.)
- What preparation do attendees need to have made, or what information do they need to bring?
- What hardware, facilities or tests do we need to be able to demonstrate in the meeting, and what does this mean for timing and location?
- When is the earliest possible time for the meeting, given the known availabilities of information and people?
- What preparation do I need to do to make sure that a decision can be taken during the meeting? This may mean, for example, working up a small number of possible actions and their implications, so that the meeting can choose between actions with known consequences. If this thinking is not done before the meeting, then it will be hard to get people to agree that the suggested action is realistic.

Unless the meeting is to be large and highly sensitive, this checklist need not be formal or written down, and it is usually enough just to run through the list mentally.

Once a meeting is defined, create an agenda. In much the same way as when planning a project, it will be necessary to put people's contributions in some order so that the information is presented coherently. Even if you are only having a 15-minute discussion, it can be helpful to outline a mini-agenda verbally: 'Could each of you explain in two minutes what is happening with this test and what our options are? Once that is clear we will agree which option we will choose.' An agenda should remain focused on the main issues. Other issues that need to be addressed with the same group of people can also be covered, but they require the same care and preparation as if they were meetings in their own right. The timing or attendees for one meeting may not suit other issues, so adding those to the agenda of the original meeting may waste time since no progress can be made on them. For this reason, multi-issue meetings tend to require a lot of planning, co-ordination and forewarning in order to be effective.

In the meeting:

- Set the scope and objectives. Make clear what is in-scope and what will be left for a different forum.

◆ Explain the agenda, making clear that everyone will have their say, and that the timing is firm.

◆ Run the meeting to the agenda. Intervene if necessary to keep participants on the topic, to stop disruptive interruptions from parties who have their own agenda, and above all, to keep progress to schedule. Your colleagues may chat in an unstructured way when you meet socially, but they may need to learn that they will be cut short if they ramble in a meeting.

◆ Do not allow new problems to derail the meeting (unless they clearly change our understanding of the entire project in a way that makes the original purpose of the meeting irrelevant). If new issues emerge, note them and deal with them appropriately; it is likely that most of them would not need a meeting with everyone here, and some would not need a meeting at all. Similarly, do not go beyond the scope of the meeting once you have achieved the objective. As with other critical chain tasks, do not feel obliged to fill the time if you finish early.

◆ Write down the minutes of the meeting. These should include:
  - date;
  - list of attendees;
  - pivotal information (note that this does not mean a transcript of the meeting;
    - information that materially influences the meeting decision should be included, but only if it was not available from other material distributed by attendees);
  - actions allocated to named individuals with agreed timing. Preparation for and attendance at another meeting to address other issues can be a valid action.

It is usually much more important that the minutes are promptly and accurately distributed than it is for them to be neat. An e-mail or, if it is legible, a photocopied page of a notebook, can contain the same information as a formally typed meeting note.

◆ If the meeting is just not making progress, you need to make a decision about what to do. Deciding to allow the meeting to overrun is an option but it is not the only option and may not be the best. It may also be possible to reschedule a more focused session now that all the concerns have been aired. Alternatively, you can test the true appetite for a decision by announcing that if no agreement has been reached before the scheduled end time of the meeting, you will close the meeting and make a decision yourself in the best interests of the project. Considerable political sensitivity is required when pursuing some courses of action, since it is often important not only that decisions are made correctly, but also that they are seen to be made correctly. If the project sponsor is in the meeting, you may find it useful to call a short break and discuss the best course of action together.

▶ Project file

▶ Rationale

All departments and individuals who have any significant responsibility run some kind of filing system. The basic aim is to reduce the time spent searching for documents and allow someone other than the author to access the information. In some organizations there may be additional requirements to create an audit trail for regulatory or quality system compliance reasons. The necessary supporting infrastructure already exists in line departments, but in projects it must be created. Without a project filing system key documents are likely to get lost. There is a temptation just to try to manage project documents in an existing departmental filing. Occasionally, this may be viable during the project but it will always cause problems at the end of the project when the project is shut down but the department is not. It is often necessary to be able to find documents from past projects after they have been closed down, for compliance or product support reasons.

▶ Process

A one-person project will need a different filing system from a large multi-site implementation involving many vendors. As a minimum it will be necessary to establish a physical project folder for hard copy documents and an electronic folder for soft copy documents. The file structure in each of these should be systematic, so that somebody new to the project can find the document they need. This can be achieved on small projects with some common-sense folders and filenames, but large projects can have thousands of documents and this makes it impractical to browse for the right document. The largest projects should use rigorous procedures for indexing and document storage, with a separate searchable document register.

The project manager must establish a policy in relation to how project documents are handled. This should address three key questions:

1 **Which documents shall we put into the project folder?** The simplest approach is to file every single document relating to the project, including e-mails, background research and handwritten notes. This soon takes up a lot of space, and depending on the nature of the work, it may become a continuing security burden after the project has been archived if any information is confidential. If any other policy is adopted it must be clear and unambiguous and should leave enough of an audit trail for the rationale behind the project decisions to be visible.

2 **When do we allow individuals to take documents out of the master project file? How do we know where they are?** There is clearly no point in having a project folder if nobody is allowed access to it, but if people remove documents from the folder carelessly, they can cause problems for others who may need access to the

same document. For the physical project folder it is sometimes sufficient to leave a note saying who has the document. Alternatively, the project manager can insist that the master version always remains in the project folder, and people work with copies. For the electronic project folder it is usually possible for people to access the project folder online and so the original document remains available. Accessing the central electronic project folder also has serious implications for document version control (see below). However, some people tend to keep local copies of documents and work in progress, and the project manager must set a clear policy on when electronic documents must be put into the central project folder. If locally-held documents are not reconciled with the master file often enough there is a risk that different parts of the project will begin to lose co-ordination.

At the end of a project, it should be possible to archive the project folders easily. Most organizations have document archiving procedures that conform to the legal requirements of their industry. Those projects that produce a product or a process that must be supported after the project has finished must also provide technical and support documentation for the group that will be undertaking this continuing task. Typically, such support groups have their own preferred format for information and it would be prudent to find out what this is and plan for it from the start, rather than discover at the end of the project that the support team cannot use the information you have been generating.

ISO 9000

ISO 9000 is the dominant international standard for quality of organizational processes. Organizations that have achieved certification to ISO 9000 have been able to show an independent auditor that their way of servicing their customers meets certain minimum standards. Certification is possible for manufacturing, distribution and service companies. All companies must be able to fulfil customer orders in accordance with published claims, but manufacturing companies must also ensure that they can show that their products were properly designed.

Opinion is divided about the benefits of ISO 9000 certification; those who have it say that it is vital in avoiding the costs of poor quality, and those who do not have it often say that it is a burdensome administrative cost that should be avoided. This second point of view is often evidence that the speaker does not understand the cost of quality failures and does not understand that ISO procedures do not need to be any more burdensome than normal good practice. Organizations that have found ISO to be expensive to implement have often done so in a needlessly complex way.

ISO 9000 certification is granted to an organization, so your project is unlikely to need to comply with ISO 9000 unless your organization has already adopted it. It is sometimes possible to set up an isolated project to be ISO 9000 compliant, but this involves setting up the project as an identifiable organization in its own right. Do not underestimate the effort involved in separating your project operations from those of the rest of the firm in this way. A project run in this way is likely to cost tens of percent more overall than one run either outside ISO 9000 or under the umbrella of a fully compliant organization.

If your organization is using an ISO 9000 quality management system, you will already have plenty of procedures and guidelines setting out how to handle documents. Much of ISO 9000 is concerned with creating verifiable records of what the customer ordered, and then ensuring and proving that the customer got what was ordered. Underpinning all of this verification and proof are satisfactory document control and record-keeping procedures. Procedures created for ISO 9000 are an excellent starting point for project procedures, and in many organizations they will have been created deliberately in such a way that projects can adopt them directly. However you run your project, you will need to ensure that your project procedures comply with the company quality manual that outlines your organization's approach to ISO 9000.

▶ Document version control

▶ Rationale

Important documents like the project plan and the user requirements document may change through the project as new information emerges. The consequences of any member of the project team using the wrong version of these documents are likely to be embarrassing and could be disastrous. For example suppliers could be told the wrong delivery dates or the wrong features might be designed into the product. These sorts of documents need to be run under a version control system that ensures that everyone is always using the current version of the project information.

▶ Process

There are many document management software packages that include version control, but most projects can get a long way with some common sense and self-discipline. On most projects there is only a small number of documents that matter and might be changed. It is usually obvious which ones they are – anything that needs two or more signatures is a good starting point.

Documents subject to version control should have their version identification on every page, so as to reduce the risk if people work with excerpts from the main document. Automatic date or time stamping is useful, but depending on how it is implemented it may not always provide positive confirmation that two copies of a document are the same. The project manager should ensure that people always use the current version of controlled documents, and that controlled documents do not get changed without due process. The easiest way to ensure that the current version is used is to publish it in the project folder on the company intranet, and require that everyone works only from this source. Some software packages have security settings which can prevent accidental changes being made to the master document. Change requests should be handled through the project change control procedure, and this will usually mean that the original signatories on a document should also sign the new issue.

All well-run projects that include a technical development component will have to run a version control process for the hardware and software so that the versions used for tests and that given to users can be positively identified (part of what is called configuration management). This technical aspect of version control is beyond general project management, but if you know that you will need to use technology version control then it would be useful to ensure that the version control method used for general documents is consistent with the technical protocol in use.

▶ Purchasing authority

▶ Rationale

Projects involve spending money. Any significant amounts of money should be in the project cost plan but many projects involve expenditure that cannot be forecast precisely at the start. Whatever the reason for the spending, it should be controlled and traceable back to the project for cost control purposes.

▶ Process

Each organization has its own rules for authorizing spending. Where the accounting system is not well adapted to projects it is often necessary to use pre-existing department budgets and do separate manual reconciliations so that project spending is properly tracked. In some organizations projects can be set up in such a way as to allow them to purchase goods and services directly.

If there are no other rules that apply, the project manager should consider how to manage project purchases. It is not a good use of the manager's time to have to examine and sign purchase requisitions for paper clips, and it is common to have a threshold for incidental purchases so that anyone on the project can get what they need without delay. Larger purchases should be authorized by the project manager and recorded as committed spending even before the supplier invoice arrives. Some projects involve the purchase of large pieces of capital equipment, and the decision to proceed with the project will have been intertwined with the equipment purchase decision. Even though the project was given authorization to buy this equipment, you should always check with your finance department and re-confirm authority before going ahead with the purchase.

> ### Common sense
>
> Project managers must keep track of the money spent by the project. This is relatively easy if your organization's accounting system is set up in such a way that the project has a separate account that is charged every time a supplier order is placed. But this is not easy to do in many organizations and it is common for spending not to appear on the project account until the supplier invoice arrives some weeks after the order was placed. This can lead to dangerously out-of-date information about the state of the project finances. The solution is to apply common sense and to run a spreadsheet (or even just a sheet of lined paper) that team members must use to record every order they place for the project.

5
planning

What do we mean by planning?

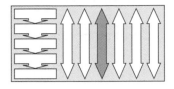

Few people who have not previously run projects will ever have had cause to plan activities in the depth required for project management, but it is one of the core tasks of a project manager. Project plans are quite different from the sorts of plans that line managers have to produce as part of their work, and even experienced line managers may find that project planning is unfamiliar territory.

This book has been written around the critical chain project planning and management methodology. The implications of critical chain for planning will be covered here.

What is a plan?

A plan is a description of how we intend to reach an objective. It is common to use the word plan to mean a prediction of spending or growth, but unless these include some description of how the growth will come about, it is not correct to call these plans in the project management sense. A plan not only says that we will do something, it also explains how we will do it.

Many descriptions fall within this broad definition of a plan. A plan can be a narrative or graphical, and it can cover events from the broadest summary to the smallest detail. Any of these can be valid in the right circumstances and it is important to adapt the plan you use in your discussions to the needs of the person you are talking to. Prospective end-users of a proposal are usually only interested in knowing when they need to give their input to the team and when their new system will appear; facilities managers might need a lot of detail on a small portion of the work; team members need to know about the whole project in detail. Given the different information needs of the different groups it is sometimes better to use different versions of the plan for each group. In such cases you must ensure that each of the plans is consistent with the others. The easiest and safest way to do this is to derive the special purpose or partial plans from a master plan for the project that covers everything that needs to happen.

Why plan?

Planning is easy to get wrong, and some people seem to believe that it adds little value. After all, if the work needs to be done, it will get done whether or not we spend time filling out charts about it.

This attitude may work for a very small operation that is unconstrained by time and money, but even then dissatisfied customers and the frustration of being constantly in a mess would eventually force most people to do some planning. In an organization with scarce resources and limited time, planning is the only way to get things under control and to optimize our activities. It has additional benefits:

◆ The process of creating a plan forces people to think about what is involved in the project and their interdependencies.

◆ It allows scheduling of usage of scarce resources, both within a project and across the firm.

◆ If there is a plan against which progress can be tracked, then divergence can be spotted and action taken before the situation becomes critical.

◆ A properly thought through plan is one of the few defences against requests for unreasonable deadlines.

◆ Breaking down a project into separate tasks, each with identifiable outputs and deadlines, allows the project manager to delegate effectively. A well-structured plan makes it easy to give SMART objectives when delegating, and hence also improves the chances that team members will produce the desired output in good time.

◆ Clearly defined individual tasks are easier for people to focus on than a whole project in which they play only a small part. So structuring a project correctly gives team members satisfying short- and medium-term goals.

◆ A plan is a communication tool. Customers, suppliers, team members, sponsors and stakeholders can get a common understanding of when outputs will be available and why certain deadlines have to be met.

◆ Without a plan, things will be forgotten, started late, or assigned to several people to do.

Planning tools

Many people are familiar with the project timeline or Gantt chart. Gantt charts are an enhancement of the more basic Work Breakdown Structure, and contain the same information as Network Diagrams (PERT charts). All of these tools are explained here.

▶ Definitions

An *activity* or *task* is a coherent piece of work taking place over a period of time and ending with the creation of one or more deliverable. A *deliverable* is the output of an activity or task. It is vital to distinguish between the activity and the deliverable, but it is easy to get confused because activities are often named after the deliverables they are intended to produce. Drawing a picture is an activity: the finished drawing is the deliverable. The distinction is important because the arrival of the deliverables is the signal that the activity has finished and subsequent activities can begin. If the deliverables exist then it is easy for the project manager to know the state of progress on an activity (it is finished). But if the deliverables do not yet exist then the project manager must assess how much work there remains to be done on the activity, and there is usually much more uncertainty in such progress estimates.

A key concept in project planning is *task duration*, which is the time required to complete the task. Durations can be fixed or variable. A fixed-duration task takes a fixed length of time from start to end, no matter how much effort is allocated. For example, lead times on specialist equipment might be six weeks, and it will remain six weeks whether we allocate one person, one hundred people or nobody at all to wait for it to arrive. Variable-duration tasks can usually be shortened by allocating more people to do the work. An example of a variable-duration task is painting a bridge: theoretically, we can halve the time required by doubling the number of diggers.

This simple arithmetic for variable-duration tasks is appealing, but it is unwise to try to apply it simplistically to most real projects. Imagine that you had been asked to manage a project to cook dinner. Some tasks are fixed duration (cooking times in the oven), but some tasks are variable duration. How much shorter would the dinner project be if you were allocated a team of ten thousand people to help you? Of course, it would take many times longer than if you had a team of three, because you would have to spend so long breaking down the work so that everyone got to do something, allocating tasks, co-ordinating and supervising. This is why project managers know that trying to speed up a late project simply by adding people may slow it down further. Adding resources can sometimes help, but it must be done intelligently.

People assigned to work on a single task together must talk with each other and co-ordinate their activities. With only two people on the task this is a relatively small overhead, but as the number of people rises, everyone must spend more and more time just negotiating with their task colleagues, and soon very little task-related work is being done. It is this need for co-ordination and communication that means every person added to a task adds slightly less than one person's worth of effort, and also degrades the effort available from those already assigned. This is one reason why it is so important for the project manager to plan projects – so that self-contained tasks can be allocated to individuals in such a way that everyone knows the exact scope of their own task, there is a minimum number of multi-person tasks, and communication overhead is kept to a minimum.

Project planners use some words in specific ways. The word *effort* usually means the number of hours or days of work involved in a task or project. It is often measured in man-days. Effort and duration are related but must not be confused. A task could involve four hours of effort but have a duration of a week if the work is spread across several days or it is a fixed-duration task. Ten days of effort could be finished after only three or four days of elapsed time if three people share the work – though, for the reasons outlined above, they might put in eleven or twelve days of effort which consists of ten days of work and two days of co-ordination time.

Another favourite word of project planners is *resource*. Resources are the people, infrastructure and equipment that are made available to the project by the firm. Resources are anything that could be used elsewhere in the firm and that should be booked to make sure that the project can use it when needed. This definition includes things like meeting rooms or project rooms, but by far the most important resources on any project are people. All projects rely on their people resources critically, and it is important to book people for the project in good time whereas it is often safe to leave planning for things like meeting room access until the last minute. For this reason, many project managers who talk about resources mean people.

During planning, the planner estimates task duration and effort using skill and experience. However, once work is executed, the duration and effort actually required may be different from what was in the plan. Hence we distinguish between planned and actual effort and duration.

▶ Work breakdown structure

A work breakdown structure is the easiest place to start with project planning. It is an enhanced list of all the activities of the project (see Fig. 5.1). The enhancements explain how the project is broken down into tasks, groups of associated tasks and sub-projects, and they also give some information about effort or duration.

Fig. 5.1 Work breakdown structure

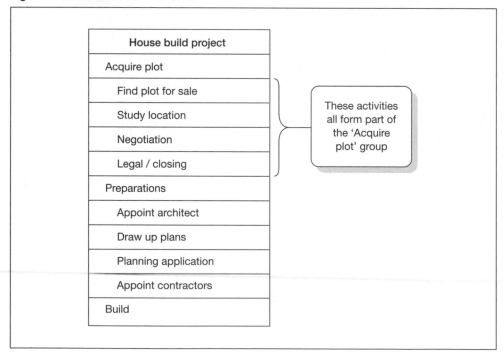

Activities which together constitute a logical sub-project or phase are listed together in the work breakdown structure, under the appropriate sub-project title.

Each activity at each level can always be broken down further, so that it becomes itself a title for a group of constituent tasks. The overall breakdown of the project into phases is given by the first level of titles, and under each phase title, the major blocks of work are listed, each with its constituent tasks (see Fig. 5.2). This process of breaking down tasks into ever finer levels of sub-tasks can continue indefinitely, and it is sometimes helpful to explore what goes on inside activities in this way in order to make sure that we really understand how much work is involved. However, it is also easy to get carried away with this process and end up with a structure with dozens of levels, the lowest of which describe tasks equivalent to 'Stand Up' and 'Open Door'.

Fig. 5.2 Excessive detail in WBS

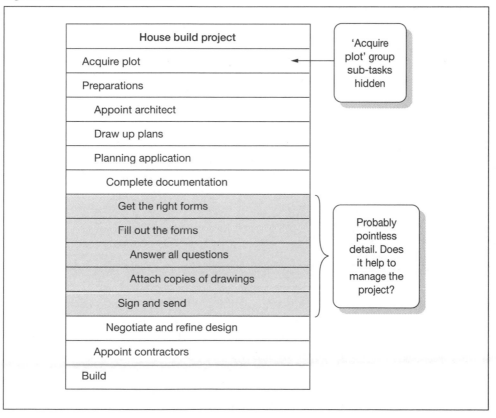

It is extremely unlikely that there will be any value in taking the analysis to this level (the exception may be in generating formal work instructions for standardized factory-like processes, but these do not really fall within the scope of an overall project plan). The task breakdown should be taken to the level where individual tasks for individual people (or for a group that works together) can be identified, with a clear explanation of all the necessary inputs and outputs. In practice, even very large complex projects do not usually need more than about six levels, and most projects can be satisfactorily represented on three or four.

Fig. 5.3 Example work breakdown structure

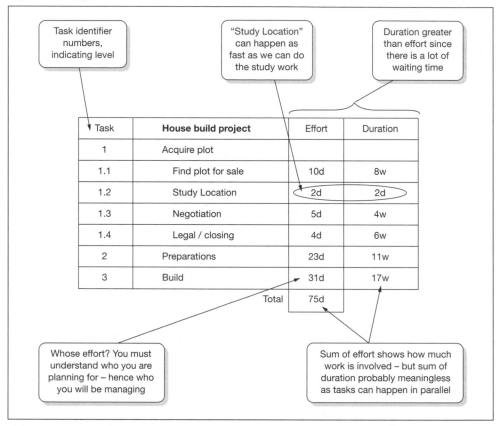

Once the list has been created, we can estimate the time required to do each task and write it next to that task (see Fig. 5.3). The times used should be the effort required for each task so that the total effort required for the project and each sub-project can be calculated simply by adding the column total. It is also useful to record task durations, especially since these will be needed when turning the work breakdown structure into a Gantt (timeline) chart. Durations should be in a separate column from effort to avoid confusing the two. Durations can be entered directly if they are fixed durations, or they can be calculated from the relationship between the effort required and the allocated resources.

It is conventional to give each task in a work breakdown structure a number or other identifying code so that it can be identified in summaries.

Most project planning software packages can produce work breakdown structures, group tasks together into high-level blocks, and let the user enter effort, duration and resourcing information. Task identifier numbers are usually added automatically.

A work breakdown structure is a convenient way to record and group the blocks of work that will make up the project but it does not contain information about dependencies between tasks, or task sequencing. There is no way to record the fact that task X cannot start until task Y (which is part of an entirely different sub-project) has finished. It tells us how much total effort will be involved but it does not tell us how long the project will take since it does not tell us which tasks must follow from each other.

Fig. 5.4 Project task hierarchy

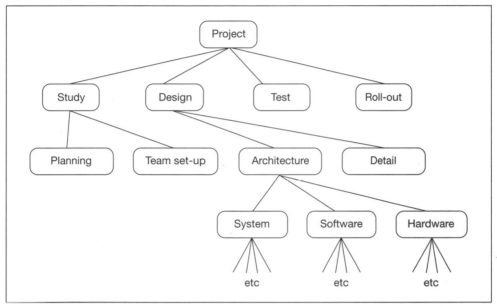

You may find it convenient and useful to represent the levels of the project breakdown graphically as well as using the levels of indentation on the work break-down structure list. This can be done easily by drawing the project structure as a hierarchy of tasks and sub-tasks, as shown in Fig. 5.4.

▶ Gantt/Project timeline charts

Once we have identified the tasks and how long each will take, it is a relatively simple step to add some information about the sequence in which tasks must happen, so that we can get some insight into how long the project is likely to take. For each task identify the other tasks that provide its inputs and which therefore must be completed before this task can begin. For example we cannot usually test a solution until it is built, we cannot build it until it is designed, and we cannot design it until the user requirements are known. In project planning language, testing is dependent on build, which is dependent upon design, and so on. This

Fig. 5.5 Gantt (project timeline) chart elements

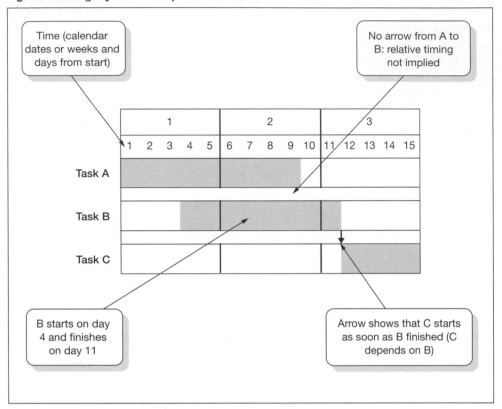

chain of dependent tasks gives us the first indication of how long the project will take. Before exploring how we can improve our view of the likely project duration, it is worth looking at how the information on a Gantt chart is presented (see Fig. 5.5).

A Gantt chart starts with the list of project activities in the same format as the work breakdown structure. In line with each named activity we draw a box on a timeline to show when the activity is planned to start and finish. Project planning software packages will do this automatically from the information entered into the work breakdown structure. This will also allow the dependencies between tasks to be defined, so that tasks appear on the plan in the right sequence. Dependent tasks are typically shown with an arrow that links the end of the first task to the beginning of the next.

Several tasks can depend on a single preceding task and a task can depend on any number of earlier tasks. Conventionally, we only use direct dependency information. If activity R depends on activity Q, and activity Q depends on activity P, then there is no point defining an explicit dependency between P and R, since it is implied through the sequence P–Q–R. However, if activity P produces an output that is used directly as an input by both Q and R, then it is appropriate to declare the P-R dependency explicitly (see Fig. 5.6).

Fig. 5.6 Dependencies

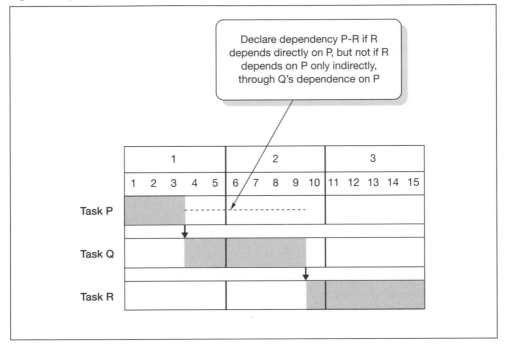

It is not necessary to assume that one task starts at the instant the earlier one finishes. Tasks can be linked in many different ways and under some circumstances you may need to define different relative timing relationships. For example, there may be a fixed interval between the end of one task and the beginning of the next, and this interval can be positive (the dependent task starts some time after the earlier task finishes) or negative (the dependent task can start a fixed time before the end of the earlier task).

Alternatively, the timing can be controlled from the beginning of the first task rather than the end, or by the end of the second task. This flexibility in describing relative task timing and dependency should allow you to represent most real-world situations, but it is essential that any relationships that you define are realistic. It is very tempting to try to shorten a project by allowing an activity to start before a preceding activity has finished, but this is a mistake if the dependent activity really needs the final output from the earlier activity before it can start. Do not dream that moving blocks around on the chart alters the situation in the real world. So, the direct finish-to-start relationship is the most commonly used because it represents the most common form of dependency between real activities (see Fig. 5.7).

When all the tasks are arranged with the correct dependency relationships you will usually find that the project branches into several chains or sequences of activities, and that these branches come together at the end of each phase. Some sequences of tasks will take longer to complete than others even though they all run in parallel between a joint start and a joint end (see Fig. 5.8). This means that most of the project branches will have some slack time but one branch – that which

Fig. 5.7 Finish-to-start dependencies

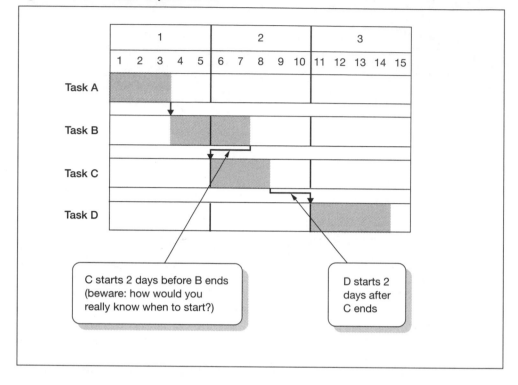

takes the longest – defines the shortest possible duration of the overall project. This chain of tasks, for which every other chain must wait, is the critical path (note that this is not entirely the same as the critical chain). It is the sequence of tasks that must happen with one following immediately after the other, without delays within or between them. The tasks on the critical path have traditionally been the focus for project planners and managers, and with good reason. Any slippage of any kind on critical path activities immediately leads to slippage of the overall project. Most project management software can identify a project's critical path automatically.

The activities that do not lie on the critical path have some slack time: we have some freedom to choose whether to start them immediately all the necessary inputs are available, or whether to wait. If they are started immediately they can tolerate some delay without delaying the overall project timing. These non-critical tasks can nonetheless become critical if they suffer a delay so long that all of the slack is used up, since subsequent critical activities must then wait for them. To make this less likely, project planners often try to get all tasks started as early as possible, even if they do not strictly need to start so early, so that the maximum possible slack is available between the non-critical and the critical tasks. This has the unfortunate consequence that during the first days of the project, when everything must be launched on the right track, the project manager must try to kick off many different activities at once. There is then a risk that the most critical activities will

Fig. 5.8 Special dependency relationships

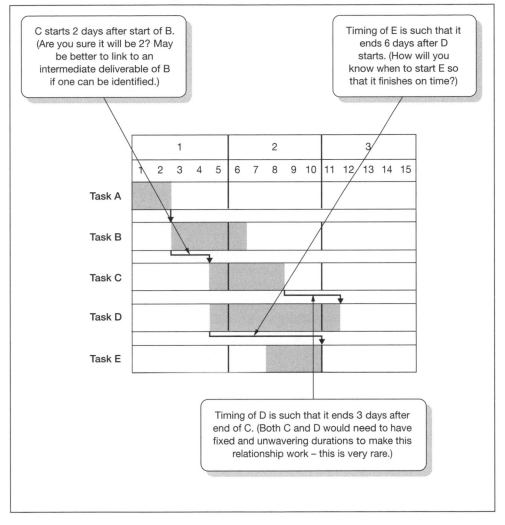

C starts 2 days after start of B. (Are you sure it will be 2? May be better to link to an intermediate deliverable of B if one can be identified.)

Timing of E is such that it ends 6 days after D starts. (How will you know when to start E so that it finishes on time?)

Timing of D is such that it ends 3 days after end of C. (Both C and D would need to have fixed and unwavering durations to make this relationship work – this is very rare.)

make a poor start just because the project manager cannot give them sufficient attention. The solution is to use the slack so that the start of non-critical activities can be delayed until after the critical ones are started. The calculations of a safe delay, which nevertheless protects the critical path, form part of the critical chain method.

▶ Resolving resource contention / resource levelling

Before addressing the critical chain safe delay calculations, we need to consider resource levelling. The analysis that identifies the critical path relies on the earlier calculations of task durations, which are derived from effort required and allocated resources for each task. But if the required resources are not available, then the task must wait. Quite apart from the possibility that resources may not be available at all during certain periods (people take holidays or are booked for work on other projects), it is quite likely that the first draft of the project Gantt chart will imply that the same people need to be working on several different tasks at once on the same project. Resources required in several places at once are said to be in contention (see Fig. 5.9).

Fig. 5.9 Resource contention

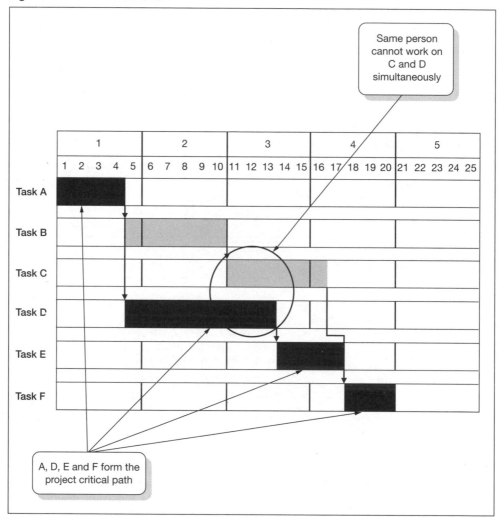

People cannot be in more than one place at once, so the plan must accept this fact. This process of adapting the plan to resolve resource contentions and ensure that resources are not loaded above 100% (over-allocated) is called resource levelling. Resources can be levelled either by delaying some tasks so that the people working on them can complete other tasks first, or by pulling some tasks forward so that resources are available for other tasks when required. It is advisable to carry out the resource levelling on small projects manually, by working out which activity delays have the least impact on the overall project. On large, complex projects, this becomes impractical and the resource levelling tool provided in all project planning software packages must be used. However, there may be no single correct solution to the resource levelling problem, and the best that software packages can do is suggest one of the many possible solutions. Because the software does not understand the project in the way that you will, you should always check whether the levelled project plan still works logically, and adjust it yourself or rerun the levelling with different settings if necessary.

Fig. 5.10 Effect of resource levelling

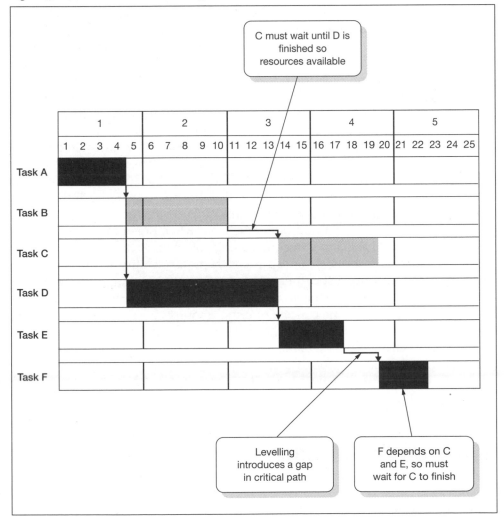

Once the project plan has been resource levelled, it will often be the case that the critical path has been broken up, with gaps and delays appearing between critical activities (see Fig. 5.10). This seems strange – after all, the software should know that critical path activities should not be delayed – but it is usually correct. The fact is that critical path activities and hence whole projects must sometimes wait until resources have finished doing other tasks. If a 2-day critical path activity starts three days before the end of a 90-day non-critical activity that uses the same resource, then the project may well be better off delaying the critical path by three days than it would be by not even starting the 90-day task until after the critical path activity had ended. This does not mean that the 90-day activity is on the critical path, but it does mean that delay in the 90-day activity delays the project. This apparent contradiction is the difference between the critical path and the critical chain. The critical path is defined only by the logical sequencing of tasks whereas the critical chain recognizes that project duration is also affected by resource availability. The critical chain includes the critical path activities and also some other activities that compete for resources with the critical path activities. So what is happening when resource levelling introduces apparent delays into the critical path is that other critical chain activities are taking place during those times. If we allow for the effects of resource levelling, the true minimum project duration is the duration of the critical chain, not just the critical path. The focus of planning and project management should be on the critical chain.

It will sometimes be found that there are one or two resources whose availability is the major constraint on project progress. For example these could be people with specialist knowledge, or a machine that is in constant use. The project can only make progress in steps dictated by the intermittent availability of these critical resources. These special resources are called drum resources, since the project progress is tied to the drumbeat of their availability. On well-resourced single projects there may be no obvious drum resource, but when organizations run several projects in the same area it becomes increasingly likely that the rate of progress of all the overlapping projects will be controlled by the availability of the one resource that all the projects need. If this happens then the project planner should try to find other ways to complete the task that do not rely on the drum resource. This is not always possible, and the concept of drum resources is very useful in ensuring that project plans embody realistic information about true constraints on progress.

The critical chain approach embodies more than an expanded definition of the critical activities, and the process of creating a project plan using the critical chain method will be explained later.

Network (PERT) diagrams

A network diagram is a graphical representation of project structure. Project Evaluation and Review Technique (PERT) is a planning method that uses network diagrams, and project managers commonly use the terms PERT chart and network diagram interchangeably. A network diagram contains the same task dependency information as a Gantt chart and one can be translated into the other. However, the timeline representation of the Gantt chart makes it more useful for communicating individual task timing and so project plans for general discussion are usually presented in Gantt chart format. Nonetheless, network diagrams are useful for project planners because it is much easier to see project structure (dependencies and groupings of tasks) on a network diagram. Most project planning software can represent the information in both ways and you should use whichever representation suits the task in hand.

Fig. 5.11 Basic network diagram

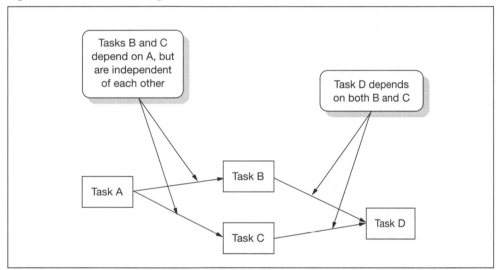

Each task on a network diagram is shown as a labelled box. A task is linked to those tasks that depend on it by arrows (see Fig. 5.11). Conventionally, the overall sense of these linkages should be top-left to bottom-right, so that the first task of the project appears at the left-hand edge and subsequent tasks flow across the diagram.

Using this representation, it is usually easy to see groups or sequences of tasks that are independent of other activities for a time, and which can therefore be set up as sub-projects with management delegated to a sub-project manager. It should also be clear where there are several parallel workstreams coming together to produce an output. The points where workstreams merge are convenient progress markers in the project, and are often designated as project milestones (see Fig. 5.12).

Fig. 5.12 Network diagram

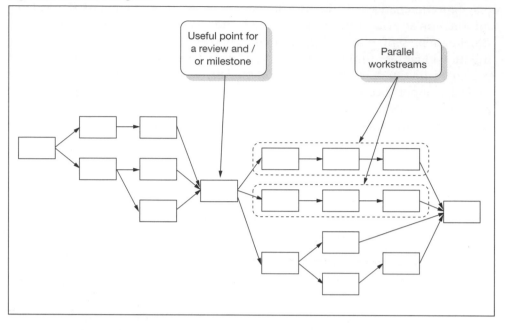

Milestones

Milestones are markers of real project progress. When the project has passed a milestone, it has taken a quantum step towards its final objective. Milestones are usually easy to explain and unambiguous: whereas there is always some margin for error surrounding statements like 'We are 32% through the project', there should not be any uncertainty when the project manager says 'We have unplugged the old system.' So milestones attract the attention of senior staff from outside the project. Within the project, milestones provide the team with short- or medium-term objectives that are sometimes more meaningful than an overall project output that can, at times, seem very remote. Letting the team run from one milestone to the next is very helpful in maintaining project momentum and a sense of urgency but milestones must be placed properly if they are to benefit the project in this way.

A common 'rule of thumb' is that a project should plan to pass about one milestone a month. This may be true on average, but it is not a requirement. Project planners who insert milestones into the plan artificially for no reason but that, or who take them out because the last one was too recent, are distorting the natural structure of the project. By doing so they risk diverting team effort from useful work while attempting to satisfy the conditions for an artificial milestone and this will lead the project astray.

Typical milestones are key events like passing tests or issuing signed-off documents. These are often associated with the end of a project phase but it is also possible that milestones can be passed within a phase. A milestone can be a significant event for one workstream but not for the others. For example, in an IT upgrade project, placing the order for the hardware may be a milestone for the hardware workstream, but the workstream that creates the user documentation may be proceeding in parallel and will not pass through this milestone. Forcing workstreams through a milestone when there is no natural convergence of workstreams at that point in a project is bound to delay one or more of the workstreams for no reason.

The PERT planning method goes beyond the graphical network diagrams to include information about task durations in such a way as to give insight into the variability of project timings. It does this using three estimates (optimistic, most likely, and pessimistic) for the duration of each task. This information is then combined across all the tasks in the plan in order to give a better idea of the possible variability in the overall project timing. It is even possible to construct statistical models of projects using this information so that the distribution of likely timings can be investigated. However, such techniques do not address the underlying causes of the unfavourable variability. The critical chain method does address many of the underlying problems, but its approach to estimating and dealing with uncertainty is incompatible with PERT. In order to avoid confusion we will not spend any more time on PERT here. See Appendix A for more details about how the critical chain method deals with variability.

Planning process

Project planning is partly a process to be followed, and partly a skill to be learned. An outline of the process is given here but if you have not planned a project before then you should try to get as much advice as possible from experienced planners before you rely on your first plan. First-time project planners typically include too much or too little detail, and may miss out work structure hierarchy and checkpoints that make the project manageable. It is easier to resolve these very normal beginners' mistakes by talking a plan through with an experienced project manager than by reading a book.

At the basic level the planning process is easy to understand: once you have defined the requirements properly you can identify the blocks of work and break them down into tasks. Next you can estimate how long each task will take and arrange the tasks systematically so that work can flow through the project. It is the detail that requires the skill and experience.

▶ Understand the requirements

Planning does not start with identifying tasks, and it certainly does not start with any planning software package. It starts with the project context, objectives and constraints. You must be clear about what you are trying to achieve and what means of achieving it are likely to be available. This means much more than just a description of the final deliverables. Questions you should ask yourself include:

◆ How similar is this project to others that we have done before and what can we learn from these?

◆ How will project success be judged? Will this be solely on the technical performance of the deliverables or will there be other, non-technical criteria applied? How should the project outputs be created and delivered in a way that maximizes the chances of success?

◆ What level of risk is tolerable on the various parts of this project? What does this mean for the amount of design and test work that is appropriate?

◆ What is the political environment in which this project will have to run and into which it will deliver its outputs? What does this mean for the way we have to organize the project and the amount of effort we should anticipate will be needed for external communication?

◆ How much do I really understand about the motivations of the people who asked for this project? Were they really listening when the risks were explained? Have they therefore signed up to the project as I think it is, or have they actually signed up to a different project?

You may not be able to answer all of these questions but you should at least think about them and try to answer them. Any that you can answer will materially improve your chances of project success.

With a sound understanding of the background and constraints you can then clarify the headline requirements for the project. Here, you should already be thinking in terms of the project manager's three-way balancing act; never forget that requirements have aspects of cost and time as well as performance. Each domain has its own techniques for eliciting user requirements and so it is not appropriate to prescribe a single approach here. For example, some new product development projects use the House of Quality framework to ensure that the development is directed towards the most important user needs, but this is unknown outside the technology area. All techniques are founded on direct communication with the end-users and if you have no other tools to help you this is the minimum you must do. So, on an internal project to upgrade part of your office air conditioning controls, for example, it may be sufficient to have some structured discussions with the facilities and maintenance department. But on projects aimed at users outside the company it is usually necessary to conduct market research to find out how users perceive the issues, and then interpret the results of the research carefully in order to extract the underlying user needs. This research programme can be a significant project in its own right, and in order to ensure that it is properly controlled some companies split the define phase into an initiate phase in which the market research is planned, and a definition phase in which the market research is conducted and the overall project is defined.

Whenever you identify a user requirement, ask yourself how you will later be able to prove that you have delivered it. Sometimes requirements are aesthetic and subjective, but even these can often be measured. An independent review can assess the appearance of something and statistical analysis can show which of a range of solutions most people prefer. Criteria such as ease of use can be directly related to measurable parameters such as cycle times or operator error rates. The discipline of establishing a measurable success criterion at the outset will make it much easier to estimate the work required and to manage the design and test phases of the project.

! Common sense

A lack of user involvement is one of the most common reasons for project failure. Knowing this, project managers devote considerable time and resources to identifying user needs. But they often run into problems if they simply ask users what they want. For example:

◆ Very few people are able to describe a product or service that does not yet exist. The best that most people can do is to refer to what they are currently using to do the job. (Henry Ford famously said that if he had listened to what his customers wanted he would have built a faster horse instead of an automobile.) So you may get some helpful information about how to upgrade an existing product line, but you will need to interpret what you hear carefully if you are creating an entirely new product or service otherwise it will end up only slightly better than the old one.

◆ People cannot be expected to be able to see how a new underlying technology will be useful to them, so asking customers whether they want different technology inside the box will not help (unless they are already buying the same technology from your competitor).

◆ What users say they want and what they are prepared to pay for are two different things. Their daydreams give you important information but your project must strive to find the combination of features that maximizes commercial benefits, and this may mean aiming at value rather than best-in-class performance.

These are the issues that occupy much of the time of product managers or civil service desk officers and marketing departments, and your first step towards a solution is to enlist the help of an appropriate person in your project as early as possible. The key in discussions with users is to frame the questions in their language and to focus on how they will use the project outputs. One technique that can be applied in many different domains is to present users with a range of descriptions of possible futures and allow them to comment on those. Depending on the audience, these descriptions can be text, or artist's impressions, or mock-ups that users can handle, or even simulated versions of the final product. The range should include something that is similar to the current solution, and you should already know something about how much each of the other ones would cost to deliver. New technology can be presented in terms of what the new design would do for the user. Note that the purpose of the exercise is simply to get users to reveal what their thoughts are about certain possible features or feature/price combinations in their own terms. There is no need to assume that the user's favourite among the descriptions provided at this stage must be adopted without further change, and the final design may well embody a blend of the various features presented.

eg Document management project

A top tier banking group wished to introduce a document management system into their Group Corporate Secretariat in the hope that it would improve efficiency and move them closer to creating a paperless office.

Representatives of the bank sat down with the software company to talk through the requirements of this new system. Over a number of weeks, many issues were covered and by the time the software house started development, both sides were sure that they knew what was required, and what was being provided. However, this knowledge was in the form of notes and e-mails and no unified requirements specification document was produced.

Development started well and elements of the system were soon being tested by the end-users. Testing soon revealed that trying to book any document back into the database crashed the system, and a period of five months elapsed while the cause

▶

of this glitch was investigated. Eventually the cause was tracked down, and development continued.

As the final version of the system was made available for user testing, one of the members of the Group Corporate Secretariat staff who had not been privy to the original discussions asked how e-mails were entered into the database. It turned out that this was not possible. No specific request had been made in the previous discussions, or in the contract, to include the ability to save e-mails on the system. The bank staff were furious since it seemed obvious to them that the inclusion of e-mails was such a basic feature that it was not worth mentioning. But because it was not specified, and because the software company did not ask the question, it was not included.

In order to remedy the situation it was necessary to spend more money on further, complex development to allow e-mails to be included. The end product was *twice* as expensive as it would have been if the use of e-mails had been part of the original specification, and the integration was not as complete as it would have been.

This is evidence that failure to adhere to a logical procedure is likely to result in wasted resources, and probable project failure:

◆ Do not make assumptions about an external contractor's understanding of your job; misunderstandings develop easily.

◆ Find out the requirements of those who will actually use the end product. If it is of no use to them, it is worthless to the company.

◆ Create a full and unambiguous Project Initiation Document (PID). If you do not ask for what you want, you have only yourself to blame if you do not get it.

▶ Identifying tasks

To identify the tasks that will need to be done, you can analyze the project top-down and bottom-up.

A top-down analysis starts by identifying the major blocks of work in the project that will eventually become the project phases. The project life cycle template presented earlier in this book is a good starting point but it is by no means the only viable project structure. Taking each of these blocks in turn, break it down into its constituent workstreams and thence into individual tasks and sub-tasks.

A bottom-up analysis starts at the lowest end of the hierarchy, with individual tasks, and works upwards by grouping these into workstreams and sub-projects. To identify individual tasks, you need to be able to 'walk the process' in your mind – that is, imagine each thing that would have to happen, and what would have to happen next. There is a knack to this but it gets easier with experience and it is helpful to use a work breakdown structure list to prompt you.

It is likely that you will eventually run into events that are so far in the future that you do not really know what will follow them. Downstream activities often depend on the output of previous activities, so distant activities cannot always be predicted accurately before work has started. When work far in the future cannot be accurately forecast there are two consequences for your plan: first, the plan will need to be updated and re-issued before work gets to the end of what can be foreseen in detail. It is often convenient to do this at the end of each phase, but if you are confident about events two or three phases ahead (if, for example, the project is a repeat of a known project) then by all means plan these in detail. The second consequence is that planning continues at a higher level. Even if you cannot plan the details of individual tests without knowing how the design will work, you nevertheless know that there will be some testing and you should block out a generic test programme that can be refined later. So as the uncertainty over the detail of future activities increases, the bottom-up approach deals with progressively larger blocks of work. On some development projects or where the later stages of the plan are uncertain, the bottom-up and the top-down approaches will both be dealing with the same high-level blocks of work in the later phases.

It is important to take a great deal of care identifying the blocks of work and tasks. A poor estimate of task effort might be 30% away from the reality, but a missing task is 100% away from the reality. Moreover, if a task does not appear in your plan at all then team members will be allocated to work on other activities. Whereas it might sometimes be possible to squeeze in an extra task by taking advantage of the padding that is common in task estimates, this is not possible under the critical chain method, since it allows no padding. If tasks are omitted then subsequent activities are left without a vital input that the missing task should have generated. This can disrupt the whole project.

To check your plan, work backwards through the list of tasks you have generated. Starting at the last task and working methodically, identify every input each task will need. Then look through your other activities and identify how the necessary inputs will be created. If you find a necessary input that is not created by an earlier activity then you need to ensure that the input is available. If it is something that should not need to be created within the project then you may be able to assume that it will be available. Assumptions should be made explicit and should be reasonable in the context of the project. We can usually assume that water will be available on demand from the tap. It may be reasonable to assume that the company intranet will be continuously available, but is this a safe assumption if the project involves supporting credit card transactions by passengers on cruise ships?

If you have identified a missing input that is not sure to be available on demand then you must insert prior activities to create that input. Watch out for teams that start work without being briefed (insert a kick-off meeting). Watch out for any activities that cannot proceed unless the output of the preceding task works perfectly. In such cases the necessary input is different from normal (it is a perfectly-working input, rather than a mostly-working one) and it will be necessary to put in some intermediate tests and rework time.

Checking for available inputs generates useful information about the activity dependencies. However, before we look at how to establish dependencies we will look at estimating task duration.

▶ Estimating task times

For each task, estimate the effort involved. If it is a fixed-duration task then also estimate the duration. If you already understand how to do all the tasks yourself then you can simply run down the list and write down the man-days of effort next to each task. In reality you probably will not be able to do this for every task, so you will need to get help from experts in the area. Estimates given by the person who is likely to do the work are generally more accurate because they have a good idea of what will be involved. When asking for someone else's estimate of a task ensure that they have the correct understanding of the task. For example, if you want someone to estimate effort for a set of project activities, it is not enough to e-mail a list of activity names and ask that they return the list with numbers added. In order to give a meaningful estimate, people usually need to know what the starting point of the task will be, what the task deliverables will be, and what the other task interfaces are – in other words, the same information you would need to give if you were allocating the task to someone during the project. The only information you should not give your estimator is any indication of deadline or timing constraints, because doing so tends to influence the estimate.

When asked to provide an estimate, most people will usually give a number that includes a large safety margin. Such worst-case estimates protect the estimator because it is then very unlikely that the task will take longer than estimated. This means that estimates tend to be at the upper end of the range of what people really think is required. Managers know this and have sometimes cut task estimates before using them, to compensate. This can weaken the manager's hand when the time comes to do the work since the person who was asked for the estimate probably feels vindicated rather than guilty if the deadline is missed.

Do	Don't
◆ Ask for a 'confident' time (90% likely), and then ask for the time only 50% likely to deliver. ◆ Get an estimate of the work involved in each task from someone who knows the area: – do not tell them the deadline; – do try to pick the person who will do the work. ◆ Take many estimates: wide scatter means the task is unclear or poorly defined! ◆ Plan for people's time in reviews, etc.	◆ Assume that management is a zero-time task. ◆ Trim durations to suit deadline without justification (reducing deliverables, adding resources, etc). ◆ Assume that reviews and sign-offs have no consequences: allow for the rework that they are intended to catch! ◆ Forget time for building buy-in.

The critical chain method offers a better way of managing estimates. When asking for estimates, first ask for the time (effort required) in which we can be quite confident of completing the task. By 'quite confident' we mean that we judge there to be a 90% probability that the task will be completed within the stated time – but an unusual combination of events could still make us miss the estimate. Once you have a 90% estimate ask for another estimate, but this time ask specifically for a number which would give only a 50% likelihood of success. This does not mean that we want a 10% probability estimate to mirror the 90% one. It means that, were the task to be repeated many times, it would be completed within the estimated time on half of the occasions. People may be cautious giving an answer to this question because they naturally do not wish to commit to a target they have an even chance of missing. So emphasize that you really do expect to overshoot the 50% numbers about half of the time and that you will not blame anyone for this. What you do with the 90% and 50% estimates is explained below.

Always treat effort and duration separately. This may require you to probe and seek clarification when someone gives you their estimate because many people will assume that you are interested only in durations. So when somebody says that it will take two weeks to prepare a document, make sure that you understand whether they mean that there are ten days of effort required or that it will take two days of effort but they are really busy and cannot work on the project for more than one day per week.

As with task identification, taking a top-down approach improves the quality of estimates. This does, however, require some experience. Project managers who have run similar projects before will have a good feel for how long certain sorts of projects usually take. They can quickly tell you that one sort of project usually takes about four months, but a different sort of project takes six months. If your bottom-up Gantt chart estimate for one of these projects points to an eleven month duration then you need to find out why your number is different. It could be that your project looks similar to the others but differs in subtle but important ways, or it could be that you could change the project plan to compress the timescale without harming the quality of the outputs. But do not compress the timescale arbitrarily just because somebody else says that it can be done sooner; remember that you have done the analysis and they have not.

▶ Project structure, control and risk

Project structure is the way the work is broken up in time and into technical areas. Most of the structure of a project should derive naturally from the work and tasks involved. By the time you have identified all the tasks and how all the inputs relate to each other you will have already defined most of the project structure. However, the plan as it stands probably assumes that everything will go without a hitch, whereas we all know that this rarely happens. So you need to modify the plan to allow better management and control, and you need to put in some risk management activities. The following points will help refine the project plan in a way that improves control and risk management:

◆ Check that you have allowed enough of your own time for your project management duties.

◆ Plan for technical reviews and general project reviews in appropriate places to check progress and re-confirm the project direction. These reviews may require significant preparation work and co-ordination but independent appraisal of the project can be very valuable as a public confirmation of progress and to ensure that the project stays on track. Remember that reviews usually result in actions, so each review should be associated with some resultant tasks.

◆ Check that the overall project breakdown into phases makes sense. Are we committing to unknown activities? When will we know what needs to be done? How can we structure the project to reduce uncertainty?

◆ Check that you know what the success criteria are. Do you know quantitatively what is acceptable in terms of cost, time, and performance? It should be possible to express the performance measures in terms of tests that can later be used to show compliance with user needs.

◆ Hold a risk review (see page 126–128) and implement the findings. This may mean building in additional checking tasks, or it could even mean planning entire contingency sub-projects to be executed only if certain risks occur.

▶ Building the critical chain plan

Having identified all the tasks, including those required for project control and risk management, link them all with the appropriate dependency relationships. Check once again that no dependencies have been omitted. Unless you check, you are unlikely to notice a line on a Gantt chart that was accidentally deleted, but a missing dependency that is rediscovered later can thoroughly disrupt a project.

Next, ensure that resource information for each task is sound. If the same person is used for several tasks they need to be identified consistently. If you know about holidays or other constraints on someone's availability, make sure that this information is used. Even if you do not know about individual holidays include at least public holidays – having to admit that your project plan failed to allow for such things as Christmas and New Year is very embarrassing! If your organization has project planning software that is linked to a central resource pool for the company then you may be able to pick individuals whose costs have been predefined. Such systems may also manage resources centrally so that the availability of each person in the company database reflects as closely as possible their known commitments on other projects.

With accurate resource information in your plan you are ready to resolve resource contentions as described above. Some project planning software incorporates features to facilitate critical chain planning, but if your package does not support this then you can do the necessary enhancements to the plan manually. They are as follows:

◆ Working with the 50% likely duration estimates, identify the critical chain of tasks that runs through the project. If your team has a sufficient range of skills you may be able to re-allocate people to different tasks within the project to avoid resource contentions, shorten certain tasks, and create a more favourable critical chain.

◆ Check your schedule to identify drum resources and see if they can be avoided. If they are necessary then you will need to structure your plan to make certain that the best possible use is made of the drum resources whenever they are available. Everything must be ready as soon as the drum resource becomes available, and this means that some other resources may need to wait in readiness without any other tasks assigned. If the source of contention over the drum resource is another project then you should insert a drum buffer. This is a block of time between the end of the resource's planned involvement with the other project and the time they can start work on your project. But since drum resource availability is your major constraint on progress, you should nevertheless ensure that your project could make immediate use of the drum resource in the event that the other project finishes ahead of schedule.

◆ Insert a project buffer between the end of the last activity and the project target delivery date (see Fig. 5.13). If the delivery date is already known this may mean that there is a delay before the project needs to start. If the implied start date has already passed then you will need to shorten the project (see below) or report that it cannot be done. A project buffer is the result of aggregating the differences between the 50% task estimates and the 90% task estimates through the project, and applying them in a way that protects the overall schedule rather than each task individually. This can provide the same safety margin as having a buffer on each task but in a shorter overall project (see Appendix A). To calculate the size of the project buffer, either:
  – take one half of the sum of the durations of the activities along the critical chain; or
  – take the square root of the sum of the squares of the differences between the 90% estimates and the 50% estimates for the tasks along the critical chain.

The second of these options is more rigorous but the first is far easier to explain and implement. If your project planning software will not do this for you automatically then simply insert a dummy task of the appropriate duration at the end of the project.

◆ Insert feed buffers in those places on the plan where non-critical workstreams join the critical chain, to protect the critical chain from any variability in the timing of the non-critical tasks (see Fig. 5.13). Calculate the size of the feed buffers in the same way as for the main project buffer, using the activities in each feeding workstream instead of the critical chain activities in calculations.

◆ Step through every task on the critical chain and identify the critical resources. These resources must be available as soon as the activity needs to start, otherwise the project will be delayed. In order to prevent delay, put resource buffers into the plan (see Fig. 5.13). These may take several forms: it may be appropriate to allocate extra resource in the form of a buffer, but it might also be sufficient to put in a reminder to check that the resource will be available some days before the task starts. If the project cost of delay is known, then it is relatively easy to calculate how much it is worth paying external suppliers to keep their resources instantly available – although we should of course initially try to persuade them to do this for us without payment.

Fig. 5.13 Critical chain buffering

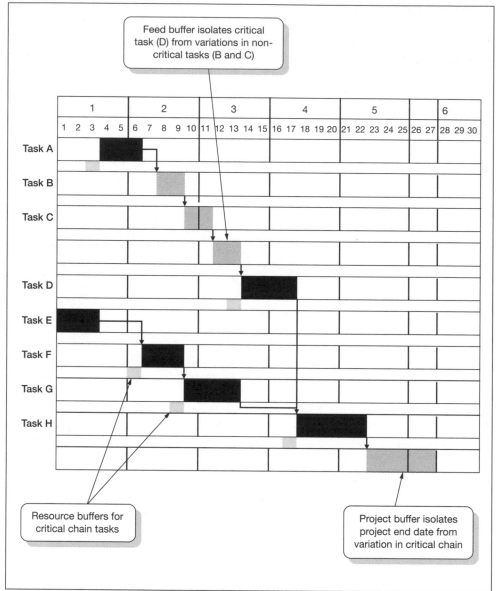

Feed buffer isolates critical task (D) from variations in non-critical tasks (B and C)

Resource buffers for critical chain tasks

Project buffer isolates project end date from variation in critical chain

Re-planning and speeding up the project

The first draft of the plan often comes as a shock: 'It can't possibly take that long, can it?!' It can and since you have just done the plan you can prove it. But this is not always a sufficient answer: just because it *can* take that long, it does not always mean that it *must* take that long. So you will often come under pressure to revisit the plan and to shorten it.

There may also come times during the project when you need to shorten the remaining part of the work in order to bring the project back on track after it has diverged from the plan. The issues here are similar to those involved when shortening a timeline at the initial planning stage. It is usually possible to compress the time somewhat, but at a price of increased risk and possible degradation in the quality of the deliverables. As always, the project manager's job is to find an appropriate balance.

> ### Common sense
>
> There is always pressure to do projects faster. There is never enough time, and somebody has always got a good reason why it must be finished by a certain date. But just because somebody wants it by a certain date does not mean that it is possible or even wise to deliver it by that date. You will come under pressure to commit to deadlines that are not achievable or realistic, but you are not obliged to agree to them. If you have taken care over the plan, you are the best-qualified person to say what is achievable, irrespective of seniority. If you have not yet done the plan and somebody gives you a target date, make it clear that you will treat it as an important input parameter but do not commit to that date until the plan says that it is possible.

There are four ways a project can be accelerated:

◆ by reducing scope

◆ by changing the structure (the relationship between tasks)

◆ by shortening individual tasks, or by re-allocating resources on critical chain tasks.

▶ Reducing scope

If time is the overriding priority then compromises will be necessary on other axes in order to meet deadlines. It is much easier to hit a short deadline if there is less work to do, so it is worth confirming the priorities of the users and the project sponsor. They may prefer to have a minimal set of deliverables early rather than the full deliverables later.

With the benefit of your insight into the plan you may know that it is just possible that the short deadline could be achieved if everything goes perfectly and none of the contingency activities are needed. People outside the project often seize on this as a commitment to deliver in the shorter time, conveniently forgetting that there is only a small probability that it will happen. It may be natural for people to hear only what they want to hear in this way but it is a test of your communication skills to ensure that everyone understands the plan and is not entering an agreement with you on the basis of false hopes. For your own benefit and that of everyone on the team, you need to be sure that if someone says that they will accept only a 50/50 chance that your output will be ready on time, they have fully understood the risks and will not be surprised if the date is missed.

With the user needs adjusted, or at least re-confirmed, you can address the structure of the project.

▶ Changing structure

The first step in any exercise to shorten a project is to look closely at the list of activities and their logical relationships:

1 **Is every task necessary?** The answer to this is almost always yes otherwise they would not have been put into the plan. But some tasks only need to be done under certain circumstances, and if you are re-planning the project part-way through, you may have better information about what is really going to happen and so tasks that were originally planned may be deleted. Before you delete any task ask yourself why it is safe to delete it now when only a few weeks ago you believed that it was unsafe to eliminate it. Without evidence to support the case for deletion, you are probably just bowing to pressure to shorten the project, and you will find that the task has to be done whether it is in the plan or not.

2 **Is every necessary task in the plan?** Strangely, one of the most important steps in shortening a plan might be inserting extra tasks. It is better to plan on the basis of all the facts since the re-issued plan will form the basis of an agreement about the future of the project and any tasks that are not included in the plan will set the project back significantly. Particularly when re-planning a project part-way through it is not unusual to have to insert tasks because of new information that has been discovered since work started.

3 **Are the dependencies valid?** Every link shown on the Gantt chart or network diagram should represent an output from one task that is needed by the subsequent task before it can start. Such outputs can be easily identifiable physical objects or documents, but they can also be information or confirmation that something else is safe to use. If there is nothing at all – not even information – flowing between two tasks, then there is probably not genuine dependency between them. So work through the plan link by link and ask yourself whether the links represent real dependency. As before, however, you may find that you need to insert some links at the same time as removing others.

4 **Can tasks be overlapped?** Sometimes it is not necessary to wait until one task has finished before the subsequent task can start. If the resources are available to support parallel tasks then this can speed up a project significantly. Usually this means that the subsequent task must start when there is only a draft version of the earlier task's output available and confirmation of the final version of the second task's inputs will follow some way through the second task. Though it is standard practice it must only be done once you, the project manager, have thought through the consequences of starting the second task with imperfect information. Consequences usually include an increase in the effort needed for the second task, as rework is likely to be necessary once the final version of its inputs is confirmed. Hence this technique works best if the downstream task can be broken down into a preparation stage, which would have to be done no matter what the form of the task inputs, and an execution stage, with content that depends on the inputs. The first stage of the subsequent task can be overlapped with the preceding task without much risk. (see Fig. 5.14).

Fig. 5.14 Overlapping tasks

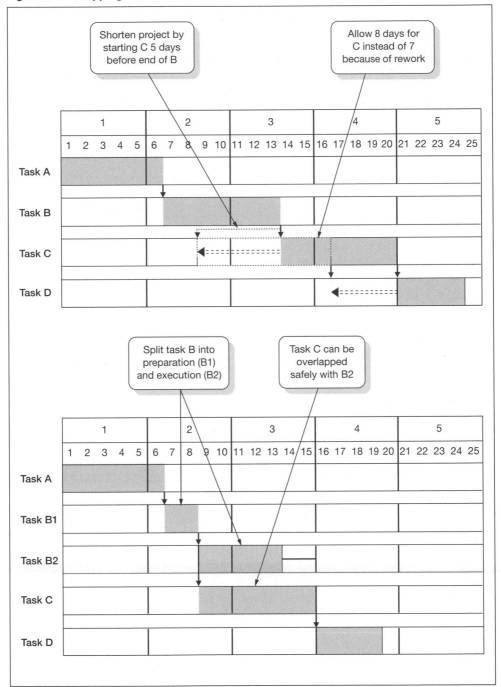

eg

Channel tunnel rail link

Though the tunnel that links Britain and France was completed in late 1994, the contract to construct a high-speed link between London and the British end of the tunnel at Folkestone was not awarded until February 1996. A consortium called London & Continental Railways Ltd (LCR) was to build a high-speed line from the coast to London and then across London to St Pancras station. The project was to be financed by LCR which would then draw revenues from Eurostar, the train operating company. Construction was expected to start in 1998 and finish in 2003.

At the end of 1997 it became clear that Eurostar's revenues were not going to be sufficient to repay the debts if the project went ahead unchanged, and it was made clear soon afterwards that the government would not make good the £1.2 billion shortfall with a grant. So the money available to do the project had become much less than originally anticipated: cost was out of balance with time and performance.

In June 1998 a solution was agreed that brought cost, time and deliverables back into line. The project was split in two: one part, linking the tunnel with the outskirts of London, would go ahead immediately, and the other part, crossing London, would be delayed. Construction of the first section is on target for completion in 2003, but completion of the entire link is unlikely before late 2006.

The LCR consortium were not the cause of the financing problem, but they had to manage it anyway. At the time they did this it would still have been possible to shut down the project without too much cost, and this was probably their next-best solution after the one that was agreed. The option simply to carry on and hope that it would sort itself out would have cost far more than either of the other options. LCR recognized the severity of the problem and redefined the project so that the new plan met the changed requirements.

▶ Shortening task durations

Shortening each task should shorten the project – if the shortened tasks are on the critical chain. Shortening tasks is often a major focus of project recovery exercises.

Reducing task durations involves re-examining the task estimates, and adjusting resource levels.

If you are re-planning a project before work starts and the original task estimates were sound then there are probably no grounds for adjusting the estimates unless you also change the project scope and structure. Do not succumb to the temptation to squeeze the estimates without a commensurate change in the task deliverables.

If you are re-planning a project part-way through, you may have better information available about the effort needed for certain tasks than when you made the original plan, and this must be included in any revised plan. Of course some of the revised estimates are likely to be revised upwards rather than downwards but it is still necessary to allow for this in the new plan.

You can revise the resource allocations using the revised estimates of effort and the consequent changes in resource availability. Adding resources to some sorts of task can speed them up, and so redeploying the project resources or bringing in extra resources can have a significant effect on project progress.

If you have enough information available it is sometimes possible to calculate the optimum amount of extra resources to apply. The extra resources can come from:

◆ getting the existing team to work longer hours on the project (freeing them up from other commitments or initiating evening and weekend working); or

◆ bringing extra people and equipment onto the project.

Both of these options creates extra cost, so comparing the extra cost with the project cost of delay should allow an easy decision to be made about whether the extra resources are worthwhile. In practice there are usually other factors to consider and the information is not clear-cut, and so such decisions tend to be made on the basis of urgency rather than arithmetic.

> **!**

Common sense

A common mistake is to try to recover a project that is in trouble just by adding more resources to critical tasks. This is a problem because people who are new to the project will take time to learn about their task, and will slow down other team members while they do so. Even once the new people are up to speed the extra communications overhead may mean that the project does not progress much faster than before unless you are able to compartmentalize the delegated tasks very precisely.

Experience shows that, in a real emergency, the only extra people who are worth bringing in to help are those who have done it before, who understand what to do without being briefed in detail, and who can be relied upon to organize themselves without supervision. In other words, you need senior people. In an emergency, you simply will not have time to provide the support and guidance necessary to get useful work out of additional junior staff brought onto the project.

▶ Critical chain resource balancing

The greatest benefits of resource re-allocation are on the critical chain tasks. Increasing resourcing on critical path tasks (a subset of the critical chain) may speed them up, with a direct impact on project timing, but changing the resource allocation on the other critical chain activities may change the whole sequence of the critical chain. These other critical chain activities are critical because they compete for certain resources with other tasks. So substituting a resource on a critical chain task might remove the task from the critical chain altogether. This is not always practical since there may be good reasons why the same person has to do both tasks (for example for reasons of continuity, lack of a learning curve, or scarcity of a specialist skill). When it is possible, however, there can be great time savings.

Ten key questions: before you start

1 Does the plan represent the time it will take to do the work required, instead of the time available before an arbitrary deadline? Yes/No

2 Does the plan include risk management activities (independent reviews, fall-back solutions, contingency plans etc)? Yes/No

3 Do you and everyone else understand what the dates in the plan mean? (Are any dates promised? Which ones are estimates and which fixed?) Yes/No

4 Does everyone who will have contact with the project understand what critical chain working implies for them? Yes/No

5 Has the plan been reviewed by another manager with experience of similar projects? Yes/No

6 Were the estimates provided by people who knew the area and who had been thoroughly briefed on what would be required? Yes/No

7 Have you planned as far ahead as you can foresee in detail and got explicit agreement that the project will be re-authorized against a revised plan once that point is reached? Yes/No

8 Is there explicit allowance in the plan for task uncertainty? (Is there a buffer to protect the promised delivery date from variations in task durations?) Yes/No

9 Have you identified the critical chain, resolved resource contentions within the project and with other projects, and put in feed buffers and resource buffers to protect the critical chain? Yes/No

10 Is the plan founded on an agreed understanding of what the end-users want and when, why and how they want it (a user requirements specification)? Yes/No

6

monitoring and control

What do we mean by monitoring and control?

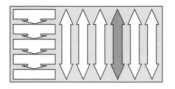

▶ Reality, and dealing with it

Failing to deliver their allocated task is *not* the worst crime anyone on your project can commit. The worst crime is having problems and hiding them until it is too late to fix them. Most problems can be solved in a variety of ways but there are hardly any ways to solve problems instantly; it always takes time. With enough warning most problems can be overcome. But by hiding the problem failure is locked in. By the time the project manager finally discovers what has happened, it is too late for recovery. It is very frustrating to know that a solution would have been possible had the person with the problem spoken up early enough.

The best way to deal with such situations is not to get into them in the first place. Much of the project manager's monitoring and control tasks centre around avoiding such nasty surprises and maximizing the warning period.

The most basic monitoring and control skills are therefore those of team building and communication. You have got to establish an atmosphere in which people feel that it is safe to report reality as they see it. This will not happen by accident since it runs contrary to many people's instinct. Nobody likes to admit that they have problems and doing so takes courage. Your reaction to the first problem that is presented to you will affect how many others you get to see. If the braver team members get the impression that you are pleased by their openness then others might be encouraged to involve you in avoiding problems before they get out of control. If the first person to tell you about a potential problem believes that you think badly of them you will not get to hear of any more problems. So shouting at people is a good way to have a quiet life for a few weeks, but then all the problems that nobody dared to tell you about will have grown until you cannot fail to notice them even without being told, and you will have a full-scale project crisis.

Your attitude in your day-to-day interactions will govern the quality of the information the team gives you. Go out and look for trouble – but when you find it, manage it like any other task. If you catch things early enough, you will be doing risk management instead of problem management, and the actions can be pre-emptive rather than reactive. In other words, you will be in control rather than just reacting to events. This is a much more comfortable way to run a project.

Information gathering

We can all agree with statements like 'The project manager must monitor project progress and take action to ensure that the project stays on track'. But after a few days or weeks of doing the project management job, it is not so easy to agree. Quite quickly, project managers are driven to ask in return 'Yes, but how? There is just too much happening. I can't monitor everything, and even on those tasks I do monitor I can't tell whether action is really required!'. What is needed is a summary of the project status, highlighting tasks that need attention.

The sponsor and the programme board face the same problem, but they have even less time to devote to each project. The sponsor cannot and should not get involved in every detail of the project, and yet the sponsor is responsible for safeguarding the organization's investment in the project and guaranteeing the business benefits. How can this be done without checking what is happening several times a day? Both the sponsor and the programme board rely on summary information generated by each project that they supervise. With the right metrics, one can tell much about the state of a project or an individual task without having to know the technical detail. The project-level summary information for the sponsor and the programme board is an aggregation of the task-level summary information used by the project manager.

▶ Task information gathering

Projects are a means to allow the necessary experts from a range of fields to work together on a problem that none of them could solve alone. Consequently the project manager may not be qualified to judge the status of much of the work on some of the tasks. Whether this is a problem depends largely on the skills of the team members, and it is always a good idea for the project manager to have enough basic knowledge at least to have a conversation with the team member concerned. Nonetheless, it is worth remembering the basic principle that responsibility and authority go together – meaning that the project manager should be able to trust the team member to manage progress on their own task without constantly seeking detailed guidance from the project manager. The manager should be able to rely on the work getting done without having to become involved in how it gets done.

The common language of task progress that allows a project manager to monitor activity in many different domains is effort (worked time): how much effort has been spent on the task so far, and how much effort remains. With these two pieces of information, it is possible to update a Gantt chart and generate project-wide summary figures (see below).

!

Common sense

When trying to get a fix on task status, it is all too easy to fall into the trap of asking 'How far through are you?'. After all, that is the information you want. But the person answering knows how long they have spent on the task so far and their original time estimate for the task, so the easiest way for them to give you an answer is just to divide effort so far by their original estimate to get a value for progress. If they have worked six days on a task they estimated at 10 days, they will then answer '60% done'. But in fact there is not enough information to answer the question because we do not know how much work is left to do as the original estimate might have been wrong. So instead of asking how far through, always ask 'How much more work is there still to do?'. If we are six days in and there are still six days of work to do, then the task is only 50% done, not 60%.

The usual way for project managers to track progress is through timesheets or an online equivalent (see 'Time recording', page 55). You should get timesheet information from all of your team at least once a week. However, some time reporting systems only record historical hours spent down to the project level rather than the task level. If necessary, therefore, you will need to create a project-specific version that allows people to record time on individual tasks and also to give revised estimates of time to task completion. On small projects, you can gather this information yourself as part of your regular Friday morning tour of the project team, without having to use another form, but on large projects some degree of automation will be required.

With complete task timing information you will be able to update the project plan and generate the summary information for the project.

> **Common sense**
>
> A sudden reluctance on the part of a team member to provide a regular progress update is itself a warning sign. It might be simple forgetfulness, but it might mean that the person is worried about the real status of their corner of the project. You need to find out not only the time information, but whether there are any emerging problems.

▶ Project reporting

The project team are not the only people interested in the project. The sponsor, the programme board, the managers of other projects that are waiting for your resources, the various stakeholders, and of course the users, are all keen to know how things are going. They aren't likely to be interested in the details that occupy most of your time but they will all want to hear when the project is likely to finish and whether everything is under control. Some of these contacts will need to be informed on an as-needed basis, but as a general rule, reporting should follow the pattern set out in the Project Reporting table below.

The two most significant reporting tasks for a project manager are the weekly note for the sponsor, and the weekly project status report for the Programme Office. The project status report is a required document, but since it contains summary information of what should already have been generated for internal project use, it should be simple to produce. Many sponsors are content to receive a copy of the weekly programme status report without any additional project progress note. However it is good practice to send a weekly note to the sponsor. Sending regular routine notes will make you appear organized, and will mean that, if your project does run into trouble, that will not be the first that the sponsor has heard about the project. Through being reminded of the project the sponsor will be better placed to act as project ambassador in interactions with other senior staff. Take the opportunity to raise issues and concerns that do not fit into the project status report format and to ask for support in dealing with any organization, political or resourcing problems that may be emerging.

As well as the formal upwards reporting channels, you should use informal channels to keep people elsewhere in the company informed about progress – particularly if it is good. When the time comes to roll out your hard work across the firm, you will be grateful for the extra supporters.

From	To	Frequency	What
Project manager	Sponsor	Weekly	Informal progress note: ◆ progress and status vs plan; ◆ achievements and problems; ◆ necessary actions.
Project manager	Programme board/Project support office	Weekly/ monthly	Status report: ◆ progress against plan; ◆ revised cost and time projection.
Project manager	Sponsor	At major milestones/ review points	Project review report: ◆ snapshot of project; ◆ explanation of project decisions; ◆ analysis of other project events and learning; ◆ recommendations.

▶ Using the project plan

A good project management mantra is 'Plan the work and work the plan'. We have already looked at planning, but how do we 'work the plan'? The first steps in working the plan are similar in most projects: assemble and brief the team about the project, and kick off the first of the core project tasks (remember that gathering enough information to make a good plan for the project may itself be a planned task). Thereafter, keeping the project running smoothly involves gathering information about progress and taking actions to keep the plan and reality in line.

It is not enough to have a plan and to ensure that everyone involved in the project understands it at the outset. Circumstances will change, new information will emerge, and people's memories of tasks and objectives will diverge. So you must keep their understanding up to date. The only way to keep a project on track in the real world is to refer back to the plan constantly, and to update that plan to reflect what is actually happening.

▶ Task allocation

Working from the current version of the project plan, updated with actual progress on foregoing activities, set your team members going on their tasks. Remember to set SMART objectives, to re-confirm people's understanding of project context, and to make a final check that the required inputs are in fact available.

The critical chain method imposes certain specific demands on the way tasks are allocated and managed. One of the hardest of these demands for experienced project managers is to refrain from specifying a deadline date for each activity. Classical project management thinking (e.g. critical path and PERT) teaches that without a deadline tasks will drift indefinitely and so critical chain is a great change for anyone who has this training. Despite the lack of a deadline in the critical chain approach, nobody should get the impression that timing does not matter. It is very important to emphasize that the work should be done as quickly as possible. (If no date is given, then there should be a fair chance that the work will be completed before the 50% likely time estimate – could you imagine that this would happen had you originally given a target date that equalled the 90% estimate?) Nothing must be allowed to get in the way of delivering task deliverables of acceptable quality absolutely as soon as they exist. In fact, this principle is so important that it drives another departure from what has historically been considered normal – in critical chain, multitasking is not allowed. Rather than trying to do several jobs at once and therefore making slow progress with all of them, the critical chain task must get undivided attention until it is finished. Because other tasks will also get full attention when their turn comes, their actual delivery dates will not be worsened, but the priority task will get done much faster.

> ### Common sense
>
> Get into the habit of carrying the current version of the PID – or at least the Gantt chart – wherever you go. Print it out and stick it to the inside cover of your daybook, so that you can refer to it if required during any conversation next to the coffee machine, or while you are walking around the team members' work areas. When somebody tells you something about how their task is progressing, you need to be able to check quickly what that means for the rest of the project tasks and hence whether you will have to do some rescheduling. It is better to give an answer immediately than to defer replying until you get back to your desk (where of course there will be a dozen e-mails waiting to distract you).

A further consequence of eliminating the fixation on task deadlines is that team members should understand that they cannot be called 'late' in the normal sense. Even if the people on your team are the same individuals who gave the original planning estimates and they can remember their '50% likely' estimate for a task, they should also understand that you fully expect them to overshoot that estimate some of the time and will not reproach them as long as they undershoot just as often. Instead of criticizing people for being late, the critical chain method reserves criticism for anyone who breaks one of three rules:

◆ people must start work on a task promptly as soon as the inputs are available;

◆ people must work 100% on the task until it is done; and

◆ people must hand the outputs on to the next activity as soon as they are available.

This book was written following this prioritization system, and it was hard for the authors, experienced project managers, to practise what we preach about critical chain. Other tasks were always being proposed, there were always distractions and colleagues wanting to know why their work had not even been started. But the book was finished on time. As the critical chain method takes hold and becomes the norm, it becomes easier for project managers trained in other methods to work this way.

▶ Progress tracking using Gantt charts

Gantt charts are both a project planning tool and a progress tracking tool. Using your project planning software, you can update the plan to reflect the latest information and, if you have defined the dependencies rigorously, all of the subsequent tasks will be updated as well, giving you the best current estimate for completion. Note that you should never just change the original data in the plan: all software packages allow you to enter the 'actuals' in another field, so that progress against the original plan can be seen. It is also important from the point of view of project authorization that the original project timing information does not get overwritten. The project authorization was granted against the original planned timing and new information about actual timing does not authorize you to change the planned dates: only a fresh authorization can do that.

Once you update the plan with 'actuals' data, each task that was shown as a single timeline bar on the original plan is now represented as two bars – one for the plan, and one for the actual. The actual bar can also be shaded up to a certain point to show the proportion of the task that is believed to be finished. Since today's date is usually shown as a vertical line, it is easy to look down the tasks on the chart and see which tasks should have finished, which should have started, and whether the progress on those that have been started is about what we would expect (see Fig. 6.1).

What makes this a useful exercise is the information it produces. Overrunning tasks could mean many different things, but the only ones that matter usually are those on the critical chain (unless something has gone so disastrously wrong on another activity that a non-critical workstream is about to devour its entire feed buffer and take over the critical chain). Once you discover that you need to worry about a task find out what is going on. Laziness or incompetence are possible explanations but they are very rare. By far the most likely explanation is that the task has run into unexpected difficulties. Go and talk to the person responsible for the overrunning task and find out what the difficulty seems to be, whether it is now under control, what the anticipated completion date really is, and whether there is anything that you can do to ease the situation. Naturally, you should be careful about how you talk to this person as any intimidation will make it more difficult for you to get all the facts. Invoke any of the other techniques of scope management, risk management, or even project recovery, that you need to use to get the critical chain back on track.

▶ Progress tracking using critical chain

With updated information about past and predicted task timings, it is possible to update the project plan as described above for Gantt charts. But the timing in the project plan was set on task duration estimates that were believed to be only 50% likely to be achievable, and a gap (the project buffer) was left between the end of the last activity and the planned project completion date. So we expect to overshoot the date of the end of the last activity as it appeared in the plan on about 50% of occasions. This does not matter much as long as we do not also overshoot the end of the buffer. Hence buffer usage is a key parameter for a project manager.

Fig. 6.1 Gantt chart updated with actual progress

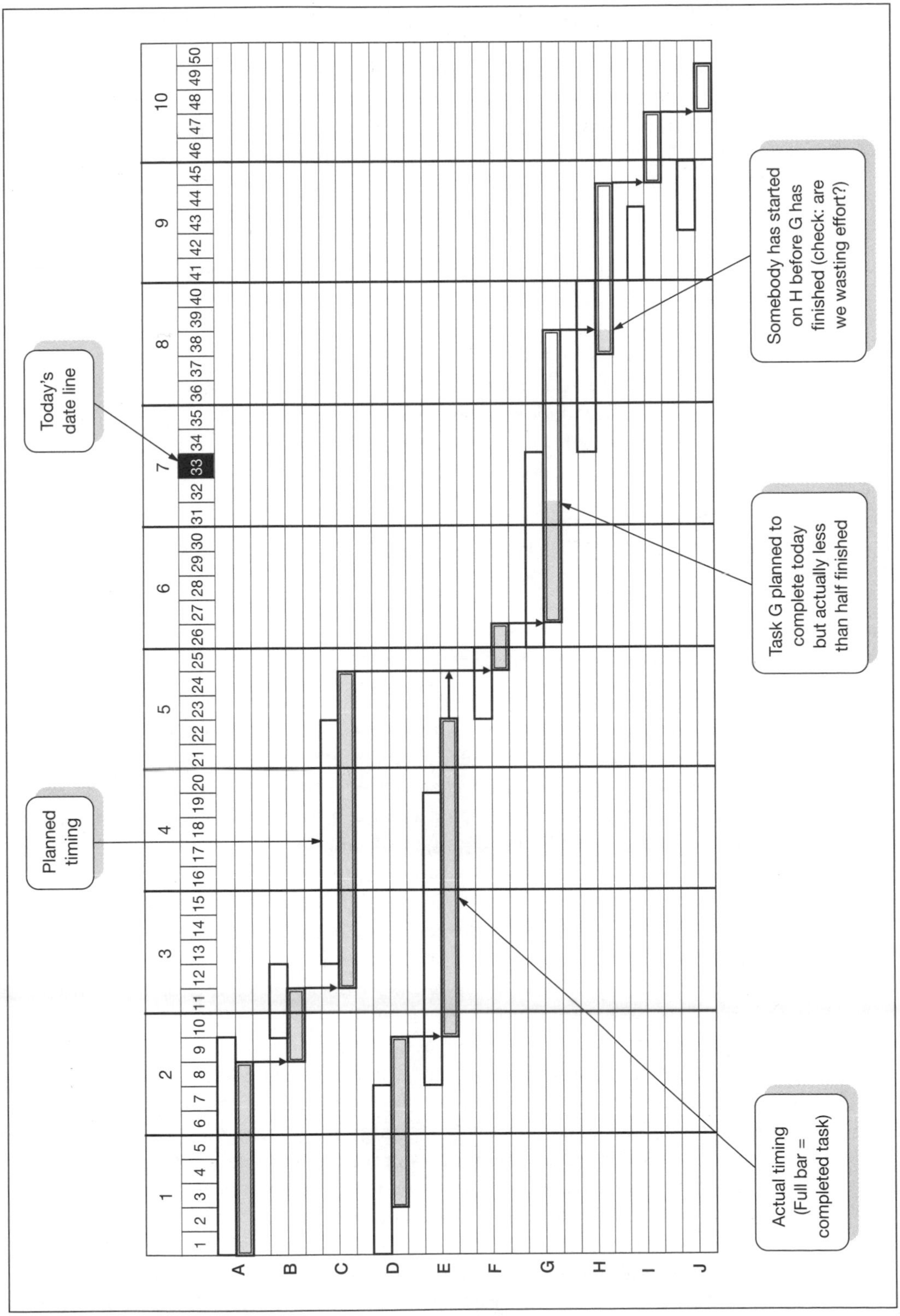
Planned timing
Today's date line
Actual timing (Full bar = completed task)
Task G planned to complete today but actually less than half finished
Somebody has started on H before G has finished (check: are we wasting effort?)
A
B
C
D
E
F
G
H
I
J
1 2 3 4 5 6 7 8 9 10
1 2 3 4 5 6 7 8 9 10 11 12 13 14 15 16 17 18 19 20 21 22 23 24 25 26 27 28 29 30 31 32 33 34 35 36 37 38 39 40 41 42 43 44 45 46 47 48 49 50

Buffer usage is easy to measure. Simply update the task timing information, your plan and calculate a new predicted date for the end of the last scheduled task on 50% probable timings for the remaining tasks. If the new date is before the originally planned one, then the project looks set to come in below the 50% timing overall, and buffer usage will be zero. (Strictly, buffer usage would be negative under these conditions, but nobody worries too much about this – it still means the project is OK.) If it is after the originally planned date, then the buffer usage is the proportion of the original buffer time predicted to be used:

$$\text{Buffere usage} = \frac{(\text{Actual predicted end date} - \text{Planned end date})}{(\text{Buffer end date} - \text{Planned end date})} \times 100\%$$

If the buffer is unused, then if any progress has been made then the project is probably quite safe. If some buffer is being used, then the project might be OK but a little more detail is needed. In order to interpret a buffer usage figure correctly, we need also to know how far we are through the project. This number is called the 'percentage complete':

$$\text{Percentage complete} = \frac{\text{Work done}}{\text{Total amount of work}} \times 100\%$$

$$= \frac{\text{Work done}}{(\text{Work done} + \text{Work still to do})} \times 100\%$$

This is a simple idea but pay attention to the definition of the total amount of work. If you want the right answer you must use 'Work done + Work still to do', not 'Planned work', for the reasons already explained in 'Task information gathering,' above. This point is important because some software packages will use planned work when reporting percentage complete, even though this is misleading. Check what your software does before relying on its answer!

Percentage complete calculations can be applied to individual tasks and to the project as a whole.

We can calculate figures for buffer usage and percentage complete, but what do they mean? What matters is the ratio of these two figures. If a project has used 64% of its buffer but is 98% complete, we probably do not need to worry too much. If a project has used 98% of its buffer but is only 64% complete, this is evidence of serious problems for which corrective action is required.

The critical chain method has its roots in production engineering and this provides the concept of a planning threshold and an action threshold. The amount of buffer you can safely use depends on how far through the project you are. The thresholds move closer to 100% usage as the project approaches completion (see Fig. 6.2).

If at any time buffer usage is positive, scale the original buffer by the percentage incomplete, to give the progress-adjusted buffer:

$$\text{Progress-adjusted buffer} = \text{Percentage incomplete} \times \text{Original buffer}$$
$$= (1 - \text{Percentage complete}) \times \text{Original buffer}$$

Fig. 6.2 Buffer usage and action thresholds

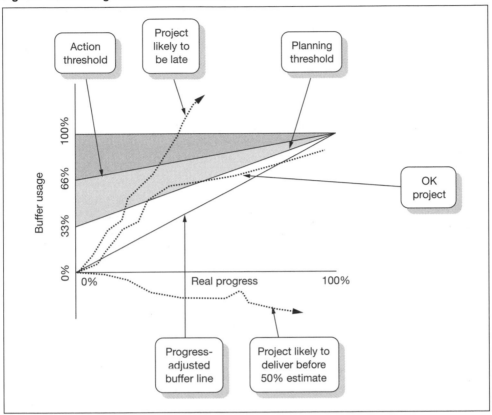

Planning and action thresholds then work as follows:

◆ If the project has used more than one-third of the progress-adjusted buffer then you should diagnose the situation and create a plan for recovery.

◆ If the project has used more than two-thirds of the progress-adjusted buffer then you should put your recovery plan into action.

This approach to monitoring the project buffer should also be applied to the non-critical workstream feed buffers, so that they are prevented from impacting the critical chain.

Using the project reports to update the plan and generate revised estimates for the project completion date is not new. However, integrating the output of this with the concept of project buffers has produced a powerful predictive management tool that can be easily understood at all levels.

▶ Progress tracking using PERT and critical path

It is quite possible to track progress on a Gantt chart without applying the full critical chain methodology, but this does not present a convenient single-number summary of project status in the same way as the critical chain's buffer incursion metric. It is possible to produce project metrics that summarize the project status without the use of critical chain. The most common of these are earned value, schedule performance index and cost performance index. Rather than risk confusion between these and the buffer incursion calculations, they are presented in Appendix B at the back of this book.

Problem diagnosis and resolution

Identification

Sooner or later in your job as project manager, you will notice that something is wrong on one of your projects. The project progress tracking tools described above are very powerful because they are forward looking: they can warn you that the cliff edge is approaching before you reach it. But they are not the only warning signals available and since any increase in the warning period will greatly improve your chances of recovery it is worth highlighting some of the warning signs here:

◆ Project buffer is being used too fast and looks likely to be all used up before the end of the work. The formal version of this is the one-third and two-thirds progress-adjusted buffer usage thresholds described above. If you have not been using the tracking tools carefully you will soon find the next stage of the same problem: the project deadline is upon you and there is still work to do.

◆ A feed buffer is being used too fast and looks likely to be all used up before the non-critical workstream is complete, thereby leading to a possible delay on the critical chain.

◆ Somebody discovers in the course of their work that a basic technical assumption on which much of the work so far has been based is in fact false.

◆ People discover that they had made reasonable assumptions about something but that the assumptions had been different.

◆ The project picks up a reputation as a problem project even before failure has actually happened. Just as a positive buzz surrounding a project is helpful, a bad reputation can damage morale and impede progress because people across the firm who are necessary to the project withdraw their support. This is only partly soluble from within the project: immediately get the sponsor fully involved.

◆ The business benefits look as though they are unattainable.

◆ Project reviews indicate that the true status and prognosis of the project are materially different from what you believed. This includes failing technical or milestone reviews so badly that the project approach is called into doubt.

◆ The user group announces that they no longer want the project output. The project may be too late, or the technical performance may be too heavily compromised, or running costs may be predicted to be too high, or there may be other unspecified reasons.

◆ Everyone on the project is having to work long hours routinely just to keep things on track. This is easy to see when it happens but it is surprising that many people do not realize that this is evidence of a problem. It is. There are usually one or two project crises that mean that people have to put in some heroics, but this is not the same as continuous, unrelenting overwork. If the team, or even one member, are having to work unreasonable hours even without a crisis, then this is evidence of a basic problem that the project manager should address.

◆ An individual or a task group just seems to have trouble delivering what they said they would deliver.

The first question you should ask yourself when a problem arises is 'Do I need to worry?' You need some kind of filter otherwise you will spend all your time putting out fires that would have just burned themselves out anyway and possibly missing the few that might burn the house down. The easiest filter to apply is whether the problem affects the critical chain. If it does not, then you can probably concentrate on other things and rely on your trusted team members to resolve the problem within their own area. Many of the problems listed above automatically affect the critical chain because they are project-wide. Problems that are presented as purely technical can be assessed for their impact on the critical chain by getting some idea of how long they will take to solve.

▶ Problem causes

Symptoms and causes are sometimes obviously linked, but often there are many possible explanations, and a whole new project would be required just to find out which is the real one. Each possible cause may have a range of underlying causes, and they might each have various contributory factors. As a project manager, it is easy to feel overwhelmed by the idea of making any kind of decision about a solution, when the possible causes are so unclear. However, if we trace the cause-and-effect linkages back far enough, we find that there are a small number of original causes that account for a very high proportion of project problems:

◆ Forget about it being any problem with team members unless something else has prevented them from performing. People usually work as hard as they can, and they *dislike* failing. If a team member has let the project down, it is not because he or she did not try.

◆ The original plan was inadequate or incomplete. Activities or dependencies were missed, and durations and resource needs were poorly understood and hence badly estimated.

◆ The plan has not been followed properly and kept up to date, so that activity start dates have been missed and resource clashes have been frequent. A common and insidious way that activities diverge from the plan is scope creep – the tendency of a project to pick up extra requirements along the way that were never part of the original plan.

◆ Common barriers to individual performance include poor skills, poor motivation and poor equipment or support. These may be hard to identify, particularly if they are compounded (for example, someone with the wrong skills chose the wrong equipment to use and does not realize that they need help). Poor motivation can be hidden, but it is the only cause with symptoms that look like 'could not be bothered' – this is a good example of why it is necessary to separate symptoms from causes. Motivation can be addressed, but 'could not be bothered' cannot.

◆ The original plan was not in fact a real plan in the sense described in this book, but just a wish list of incompatible requirements and dates. This can happen if the project has been created informally without the proper planning process to ensure that what is promised can be delivered. A common subset of this cause is the impossible user requirement. Again, this is easy to let slip through unless the definition phase has been rigorous.

◆ Senior managers do not give the project their support, with the result that it does not get access to the resources and facilities it needs, and the final project output will be at risk of rejection. Though this is essentially a political problem outside the project, it is still your responsibility as project manager to do what you can for your project.

▶ Finding solutions

Once you have a good idea of what is going on and why, the solution to problems in the project may be clear. But if it was that easy your team members would probably have sorted it out themselves and you would never have heard of it. So, many of the problems that you will see will need careful thought before a workable solution can be found. Time constraints will often rule out the obvious way forward. For example, if the deadline is only two weeks away and the only person on the project who knows about the software finally admits that they are out of their depth then the obvious solution of a training course is not workable.

Finding solutions is all about making trade-offs and compromises. The only thing you can be sure of is that something will have to give. Maintaining the correct project balance between timescales, quality of deliverables, costs and risks will usually mean that a solution must address each of these dimensions. This is both a problem and an opportunity. It is a problem because anything that you do to solve a timescale problem, for example, is likely to have cost, performance and risk consequences. It is an opportunity because seemingly insurmountable problems in one dimension can be overcome by changing the others. For example, a project cost problem might be easier to solve by adjusting project timescale or deliverables than it would be by attacking it head on as a pure cost issue.

So lateral thinking will help. You have got to find a solution that keeps overall time, cost, risk and final performance in balance. You will find that much of your time will be spent resolving everyday project problems in this way. The vast majority of these can be resolved within the scope of the project – this is the reason for having a project planning process that recognizes uncertainty and includes a project buffer. However, some problems cannot be resolved within the boundaries set out in the PID or within other commitments. Solving these kinds of problems requires more communication and negotiation with people outside the project boundaries. The compromises needed to keep timescales, cost, deliverables and risk in balance may require their agreement.

All changes to the project that affect the agreed scope, timescale and cost must be subject to the scope management procedure (see page 120).

Common sense

First Rule of Hole: 'When in a hole . . . STOP DIGGING

If your project is not going to plan, and there is not some clearly identifiable cause that you are sure has now gone away, then just carrying on will not solve the problem. When the project gets into trouble, the temptation to try to solve it by simply working harder is often overwhelming, but this may be the worst thing to do, since by do doing so you will be consuming time and money that might be better spent on the project recovery that will eventually be needed. If the project is heading away from the track, then just pushing ahead will send it further off the track! See Fig. 6.3.

Fig. 6.3 Problems need to be confronted

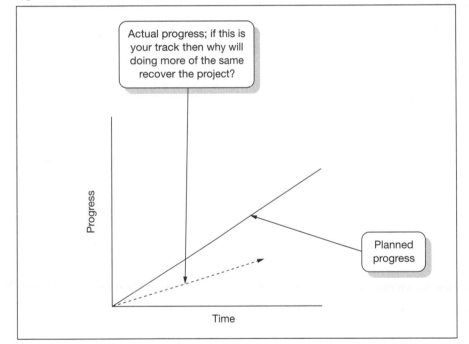

So if you realize that there is a problem, stop and think. If changes need to be made, make them. Most of the time, this will mean just pausing for a few minutes to think through what is actually going on. But in extreme cases, when the project is at an impasse, it might even be necessary to stop all further project work until agreement is reached. After all, there is no point proceeding with a project that cannot reach its current objectives, and stopping work temporarily can give you a breathing space to re-plan the work while adding urgency to the necessary negotiations.

> **Five Steps for problem resolution**
>
> 1 Acknowledge that there is a problem.
>
> 2 Find out what is going on.
>
> 3 Find out why.
>
> 4 Agree a solution to get deliverable and target back in line (change either or both.
>
> 5 Follow change management procedure.

▶ Reviews, reporting and control

Trying to tackle every project problem by yourself can make you feel isolated and lonely. The need to give the project team clear objectives and solutions can be at variance with the basic uncertainty inherent in some situations. Resolving such uncertainty is part of the project management job but it does not have to be done alone. There are two formal support structures that you can use, and as many informal ones as your personal contact network can provide. The two formal structures are the upwards reporting chain, and project reviews.

It may seem that the upward reporting chain exists only to burden you with the additional administrative task of producing regular progress reports, but in most organizations the sponsors and the programme board will give guidance and recommend actions in return for the information you provide. At the level of the programme board, this usually means calling for and approving recovery plans, but more direct support should be available from the project sponsor. The sponsor can provide a sounding board for suggestions and can add much value in comparatively little time by using their experience, challenging your assumptions, and maintaining the decision-making focus on the business objectives in the face of distracting detail (see Fig. 6.4).

The project support office can also provide useful support and guidance. It can help resolve resource problems, comment on reworked plans before they are put forward for approval, and make suggestions for project structure.

Project reviews are another mechanism by which project managers can get help from other experienced managers. When planning your first project, you may doubt the value of such reviews and seek to avoid having them in your plan, but after your first project disaster (most managers have one sooner or later), you may realize that a little friendly advice in a review can save a lot of trouble. It does take some courage to ask for a full and open project review, because the purpose of the review is to catch problems that you might have missed. Nonetheless, your reviewers are there to help and your project will be the better for their advice.

If you need to review a particular aspect of the work but it is not convenient to wait until the next scheduled project review, it is of course possible to call for a meeting to discuss just a single topic, and one or more advisors from outside the project can be invited to attend if required.

Fig. 6.4 Project reporting and control flows

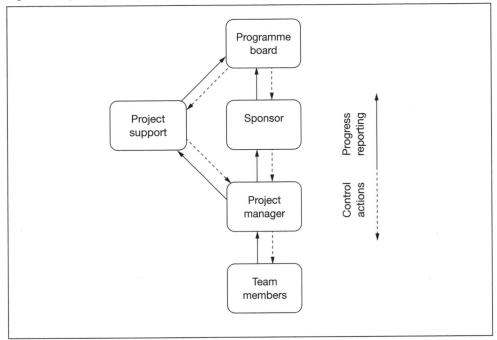

7

scope management and risk management

1
2
3
4
5
6
7
8
9
10
11

Scope management

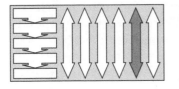

Scope creep

Sooner or later, every project manager develops some finely tuned antennae that are constantly listening for phrases like 'It would be much better if . . .'. These phrases have a nearly-magical power to derail a project, and letting any instance slip through unchallenged can have dire consequences. When people say things like 'It would be much better if. . .', they are often about to suggest changing the scope of the project. The suggestion could be to do with timing or, more likely, the performance of the deliverables, but the common theme will be that the result will be clearly better and this makes it very easy to agree with the suggestion. It would be foolish not to agree to make things better, wouldn't it?

The problem with scope creep is not that any of the suggestions are bad: they are usually entirely reasonable. The problems arise because accepting the suggestion implies changing something about the project objectives, and so the plan and the resources and all the other things that were so carefully matched to the original objectives are suddenly incompatible with the new objectives. Unless it is properly managed, scope creep leads to trouble in one of two ways:

◆ either the suggestion is accepted and the project is committed to do things that were not in the plan, usually leading to cost and time overruns, and/or compromised technical quality; or

◆ the suggestion is automatically rejected and the firm loses an opportunity somehow to improve the returns on its investment in the project.

This seems like a no-win situation. The escape route is a scope management process that allows you to keep the project objectives and project plan in line; suggested changes can be accepted but only if the consequences for the plan are also accepted.

Before applying the scope management process, it is first necessary to recognize the dangerous suggestions. They can come from all sorts of directions, for example:

◆ Other staff within the firm might spot parallels between what this project is seeking to achieve and their own needs. A slight modification or enhancement to this project could make it solve a second group's needs in addition to the original user group, and it might be much more efficient to satisfy this second group this way than to run an entire project for them alone.

◆ Another common source of problems is the insertion of intermediate target dates or extra intermediate deliverables. These can greatly increase the return on a project investment, but adding a second set of user requirements part-way through often sets the whole project back almost to the beginning, while trying to produce additional mock-ups of the output in time for a public relations event can stop everyone on the team from working on the real outputs.

◆ Project team members are one of the most creative sources of scope creep. People will always try to do their best for the project and for the customer, and it is often hard to get people to understand that delivering output that does no more than meet the requirements is acceptable. Sometimes the behaviour amounts to technical showing off, but it often comes from a sincerely held belief that they know what is best for the end-users, despite what was written in the user requirements.

◆ End-users can easily introduce scope creep through their feedback on early previews of the project outputs. Non-specialists can have genuine difficulty envisaging a solution before the project starts, and so despite the best efforts of everyone during project definition, users sometimes realize what they themselves want only once a trial version is in their hands. Furthermore, if users get enthusiastic about the project, they can quickly generate a long list of extra things that it should do in order to give them even more benefits. Any and all of these changes to the original project scope may be necessary – but we do need to recognize that scope and effort (and hence cost and timescale) are directly related.

◆ External suppliers can suffer from the same temptations to over-engineer a solution as internal team members. They can also cause problems when they provide cost and time estimates during the definition phase that are based on their own internal capacity at the time the estimates were generated. By the time the project is authorized and the order is placed, the supplier may have other work and so the contract must be given to other suppliers (involving an increase in the supplier management task), or the work taken back in-house (a clear change in the assumptions of work boundaries).

◆ Legal or regulatory change can alter the nature of allowable project outcomes overnight. The need to stop and re-plan and to re-confirm that the new project is still attractive is usually obvious under these circumstances.

One of the most common features of runaway projects is that the objectives that are being pursued no longer correspond to those written down in the PID. So every time that you hear anyone discussing doing things differently from the way you thought they were described in the PID, alarm bells should sound.

!

Common sense

The project manager cannot be the only one responsible for monitoring and preventing scope creep. Whenever a task is delegated to a team member, the responsibility for protecting that little part of the project scope must also be passed along too. Project team members must be vigilant in their interactions with users, suppliers and other members of the firm to ensure that they do not agree to actions that commit the project to stretched scope. They must be aware of and follow the project scope management procedure.

The issue log

The project manager needs a means of keeping track of all the open questions on the project. This is provided by an issue log. If there is no technical change control procedure being applied, then this is the place to log the suggested changes to the project scope. However, the issue log includes more than just a list of suggested scope changes; it should also contain the questions that need to be answered for the planned activities to proceed.

A project issue should be phrased as a closed question: one with a yes/no or numerical answer, or at least one that can only have one possible interpretation. So 'How should we proceed?' is not a suitable question, but 'Should we take approach A or approach B?' is. The very act of formulating a suitable statement of the problem for the issue log is an important step towards a solution. You will often find that what you thought was only one problem needs to be decomposed into two or more separate issues, and so the discipline of adopting the issue log format makes the task of delegating the job of finding answers easier.

Tasks delegated from the log should be assigned to named individuals in the usual way. The log should then be used to record the answer, or at least to record where in the project file a full explanation of the answer can be found.

Use the issue log as a day-to-day reminder of what the important questions are. Add to it when new questions arise, and mark issues as closed when an appropriate answer is found. So when someone suggests a change to the project scope, the issue is 'Should we adopt this change?'.

For convenience, the issue log is usually set up as a spreadsheet with the following columns:

◆ **Issue number** – a unique number, for identification purposes.

◆ **Issue type** – change request, or establishing acceptability of deliverables of a certain status, or clarification of technical or user requirements.

◆ **Originator** – who identified the issue (in case someone needs to go back to the originator for clarification).

◆ **Date identified.**

◆ **Description of the issue** – the closed question that will tell us what to do. Be sure to make explicit reference to the exact version of any relevant documents or hardware/software, so that there is no doubt about what the question refers to.

◆ **Current status** – who is assigned to deal with the issue, and whether it is closed or open.

The issue log itself should be subject to some form of version control so that there is no risk that different people in the team can have different understandings of the project issues.

At the end of the project, during the review phase, the issue log forms a convenient record of how the project proceeded, and why certain decisions were taken. There should be no open issues left at the end of the project: either the project is finished without answering the question (in which case the question was not a relevant one for this project), or the project is not really finished.

Scope management process

Technology development projects will usually have a scope management process (often called configuration management) to control the version of the hardware and software that is tested and then distributed to users. It is beyond the scope of this book to try to describe a technology scope management process that would be suitable for use in all circumstances and can supplant those systems already in use. What is described here should be suitable for change control in general projects and should be broadly compatible with most technology change control protocols. The focus of this process is on managing changes to the project as defined in the PID. For example, changes in:

◆ target completion date for the project;

◆ project costs;

◆ quantity, quality and performance of the project deliverables, i.e. changes to the user needs.

Changes to project risks are only addressed here insofar as the risk management process may generate risk management actions that require changes in timing, costs or deliverables.

From the instant that the PID is authorized, the scope of the project is frozen. Any information that implies that the actual project and that defined in the PID will be materially different should trigger the scope management process.

The general process should run as follows:

1 Whenever an action is proposed, consider whether it constitutes a change to the project scope. This is easier to do if you carry a copy of the PID with you wherever you are.

2 Get a written description of the proposed change, with as much clarity as possible. Ideally, the originator should describe the new objectives but you will often find that you will be the one writing down someone else's idea. If this is the case, try to remain neutral and try not to let your views colour what you write. You may find it helpful to list exactly which paragraphs of the PID would need to be altered, and to provide an alternative text. Check this summary with the originator to confirm that it captures their idea, but make clear when doing so that this does not mean that the idea is accepted. Some proposed changes will come from your own analysis of the state of the project and the actions necessary to keep the project in line with the target. Treat these the same as other proposed changes.

3 Go back to the project plan and work out the consequences of accepting or not accepting the change. Focus on timescales, costs, performance of deliverables, and risk. If there are many suggested changes then it will be impractical to repeat this exercise for every one. Under these circumstances, group the suggested changes logically and produce project scenario plans in which one or more group can be actioned independently. It may become clear at this stage that some suggested changes clash with project priorities. For example, they may imply accepting a delay in project completion that is incompatible with hitting a target launch date that is controlled outside the firm. If this is the case, then such changes should be rejected. A good compromise if they are otherwise good ideas is to record them and revisit them once the core project is finished with a view to initiating possible spin-off projects.

4 Discuss the results of the re-planning exercise with the originator of the idea and ensure that they understand the consequences of their request. If the originator decides not to pursue the request at this point then record the decision and move on. If the suggestion would lead to an improvement in the project (lower cost, shorter time, better deliverables etc.) without any other drawback then it can be accepted immediately. Update and re-issue the necessary documents, making sure that everyone necessary knows about the change. But usually the suggestion will have a drawback. Discuss this with the project sponsor in the same way as when generating the initial PID. If the change would mean that the project still makes commercial sense then, depending on procedures in your organization, the sponsor may be able to authorize the extension to the work immediately, or a revised PID may need to be submitted to the programme board for re-approval. The revised PID should make clear:

◆ the new view of likely business benefits, with or without the change; and

◆ the new view of requirements for resourcing, funding and time, with or without the change.

5 The programme board will compare the revised PID, and the business pay-off implied by the with-change / without-change figures, with other ways that the firm can spend its money and resources. If the change is justified then it will be authorized. Sometimes, when the change is a recovery plan that will increase the cost and time of the project beyond that originally planned, the realistic choice for the board is between accepting the change or cancelling the project. If your project gets through this stage and is re-authorized, you can be assured that the firm is committed to the new project and the funding and resourcing required.

6 If a change is accepted, then relaunch the project. Ensure that all team members and other relevant stakeholders know of the new objectives and plan.

Risk management

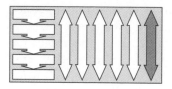

A project risk is a crisis that has not happened yet. Experienced project managers know that risk management is preferable to crisis management – it leads to fewer late nights and ruined weekends. Furthermore, hours spent on risk management are much less stressful than the same number of hours spent on crisis management. The project manager tends to feel in control of risk management activities, but one of the things that makes a crisis uncomfortable is the feeling that the project is out of your control and that you are being driven by events instead of driving them.

The personal motivation of project managers to avoid stress contributes to sound project management, but project risk management also has more direct and tangible business benefits. Solving problems takes time and money, and if risk management can avoid some of the problems then it is worthwhile. Even problems that cannot be completely avoided can often be mitigated at lower cost if a little planning is done before they arise. Furthermore, uncontrolled project risks introduce unpredictability into the firm's cash flows that increases the firm's cost of doing business. Hence it makes sense for the firm to provide funds and resources for a small additional project management task.

You may hear people argue that 'We cannot predict the future. So we cannot plan for events that may never happen. Anyway we will probably miss the problems that will really cause trouble so risk management is not worth doing.' But in fact we can often predict much of the future accurately enough and most people have a good instinct for the sort of events that are likely to happen. Furthermore, the fact that we might still be surprised by events is no excuse not to take precautions against those that can be foreseen.

Project risk management protects the business by taking a dispassionate view of what might go wrong and what can be done to limit the likelihood and impact of such events. This approach leads to the steps outlined here: first the sources of risk must be identified and sized, and then prevention and control measures must be put in place.

Sources of risk

Building up a list of the risks on a project is the first hurdle in risk management. It is very hard to manage risks that have not been identified.

It can be difficult to get started identifying risks, because the job can seem overwhelming – after all, anything could happen, couldn't it? In fact, risks can be grouped under headings, the significance of which for an individual project is much easier to see. One convenient way of analyzing risks is by grouping them as business risks, project risks and task risks.

▶ Business risks

These are threats that affect the organization as a whole in some way that may impact the project. Examples include:

◆ Changes in market conditions that may alter the commercial attractiveness of the project.

◆ Emerging project investment opportunities that may compete with this project for resources.

◆ Constraints on business activities for legal, regulatory or environmental reasons.

◆ Possibility that the market was misjudged – the project might meet all its targets, but customers might not buy.

◆ Public opinion of the firm's brand, which may limit or enhance the range of activities that the firm wishes to be seen to undertake.

Some of these are beyond the control of the project manager, but all can be monitored and the project steered round them if they are identified in time.

▶ Project risks

These are risks that apply across the project, rather than on specific activities. Examples include:

◆ User acceptance risk.

◆ Security and confidentiality.

◆ Management support and advocacy.

◆ Missing tasks or hidden dependencies in the plan.

◆ Failure of a subcontractor to deliver satisfactorily.

◆ Uncertainty about user requirements.

◆ Mismatch between the skills required and the workers available in the firm.

◆ Technology risk – the possibility that the technology will not work as anticipated.

◆ Lack of relevant experience successfully executing similar projects.

◆ Personality clashes within the team.

◆ Degree of innovation required and consequent uncertainty over whether the chosen approach will work.

◆ Timescale risk – the possibility that the output may appear after the project deadline.

◆ Project cost risk – the possibility that the funding required to complete the project exceeds that originally planned.

◆ Output quality risk – the possibility that the project output fails to meet expectations. This includes many technical risks, but also risks such as the usage cost of the project output being too high, or the performance being too low, or the quality being too variable.

The project manager can have influence over every one of these, but most of them are easier to influence at the planning and definition stage than they are once the project is running.

Task risks

Many of the project-level risks are mirrored at the level of individual tasks within the project. Individual tasks can suffer from uncertainty about requirements, or cost, timescale or quality risks. The uniquely task-level risks are those that relate to the particulars of each task, and so they are very varied. However, by tackling each task separately, it is usually clear what the risks are for each one. This is where technical risk comes to the fore: many tasks can only succeed if the technology or process under development performs as currently envisaged. Technical failure can have direct consequences for the task, and therefore the project.

▶ Risk control

There are only five possible ways to handle an identified risk: prevention, reduction, transference, contingency and acceptance.

▶ Prevention

Measures can be put in place to ensure that the risk does not arise, or, if it arises, that there is no impact on the project.

▶ Reduction

Measures can be put in place to limit either the probability that the risk occurs, or the impact if it does occur, or both.

▶ Transference

In some instances, it is possible to transfer the impact of a risk to a third party, so that if it does occur, there is no impact on the project. This is commonly done through the commercial terms of subcontractor contracts which can include penalty clauses to cover the costs of getting the work done elsewhere. Other risk transference tools include insurance contracts.

▶ Contingency

It is prudent to have plans and resources ready in case a certain risk does occur, so that there is no time lost in dealing with it. Of course, if the risk never arises, the money is not spent and the resources can be used elsewhere.

▶ Acceptance

Many of the risks identified will be either too improbable or too low in their impact to worry about. These risks should not be completely ignored since they can grow in probability and impact as time goes on, but it is normal that such risks should be logged and periodically reviewed.

eg

Critical product risk for medical device

Some pharmaceutical drugs can be delivered in the form of pills, but many need to be injected or inhaled in order to be effective. In the case of drugs that people must take every day this often means that they need a delivery device to deliver the right amount of compound in the right way. Designing such delivery devices is not easy, but it is important because some of the drugs are extremely potent and so it would be dangerous to deliver too much or too little, even though the devices are used by a wide range of patients. So as well as developing the drugs, pharmaceutical companies must be very skilled at developing delivery devices that behave consistently, no matter how patients handle the device.

One such pharmaceutical company had a class-leading drug delivery device that could handle new compounds, cost less to make than competing products, and was far easier for patients to use correctly than other devices. Of course, the product was a huge success and the company soon had orders for hundreds of millions of devices a year.

But the company found a problem with their device. Under some circumstances drug compound could build up inside the device and this build-up could be released as a single large dose some time during use. This was a disaster waiting to happen. If a single device loaded with one of the more powerful drugs failed in this way, it could cause the immediate withdrawal of the licence for the device, destroying not only the revenues from that drug but also that from all others that used the new device. The company needed to solve the problem with the device fast – so fast that the announcement that it would soon be obliged to make could also contain the news that the problem had been solved.

The resultant project operated under exceptional time pressure and with an absolute priority on solving the problem. Understanding that making an announcement without news of a solution would destroy much more value for shareholders than the cost of any amount of technical investigation, the company kept the project scope in balance by relaxing constraints on spending in this special case. The project team were given clear instructions that finding a solution was the top priority. An early risk analysis showed that there was no way to be sure that any of the obvious solutions could be proved in time, and so instead of building only the obvious solution the team designed, built and tested every solution that they could imagine, thereby minimizing the risk that the correct one would be missed. The project was a success; the business was saved and no patients were harmed.

Many risk management actions may involve a combination of two or more of these actions. For example, it may be preferable to take some risk reduction actions in order to get favourable terms for insurance against a certain risk. Similarly, contingency plans may include an element of risk reduction.

▶ Risk management process

▶ Risk management workshop

The most efficient way to get risk management into the core of the project is during the initial project planning work. Once a draft project plan exists with reasonable visibility of the detailed tasks, call a meeting to assess the project risks. Attendees should include people who have been involved in the planning and also one or two other experienced project managers who can highlight pitfalls and suggest solutions.

The meeting should aim at least to produce a ranked list of all the identifiable risks for the project. Unless the project is large, there are unlikely to be more than a few tens of business-level and project-wide risks, but if you include risks on each of the tasks you may find that the list stretches well beyond a hundred – so do not try to fit the meeting into a one hour slot.

Each identified risk should be recorded and ranked for its severity. Severity is the product of the likelihood of occurrence of the risk and the impact if it occurs. There are many possible ways to do this, but for most projects it is sufficient to rank each of risk probability and impact as either high, medium or low. The probability that you will be hit by a meteorite while working on the project is low, but the impact is high. The probability that the bus that takes you home from work will be late at least once during the project is high, but the impact on the project is low.

	Probability	Impact
High	Can be expected to occur sooner or later.	Significant impact on the ability of the project to meet its objectives.
Medium	May or may not happen, with a non-negligible likelihood.	Some impact on project objectives – may be manageable within buffer.
Low	Unlikely to happen, but may still be significant.	Annoyances. Can be overcome with some extra work.

If you feel that this does not give sufficiently fine resolution, you can use a five- or even a ten-point scale for probability and impact, but in practice this sometimes leads participants into spending too long arguing the finer points of a particular rating and never covering the full list.

In the meeting, start by explaining the background of the project, its objectives and its constraints, so that everyone knows the context. Then start to identify the risks. Consider business risks first, then project risks, and finally tackle task risks by stepping through each task on the plan and discussing risks in detail. However, it is in the nature of such discussions that overlapping risks can be raised at any time, so be flexible. You may wish to insist on agreeing a probability and impact for each risk as it is identified, or you may wish to get the list of risks in full and then return to each risk to judge probability and impact. Whichever way round you choose to run the session, it is important that nobody gets the impression that they are being picked upon just because the group has identified risks in their part of the project. Nobody should feel they have to defend themselves in the meeting. Risks identified in this meeting are a good thing and should not be cause for defensiveness. If handled properly, the risk review meeting can be a safe forum for people to speak frankly about their concerns for the project in a way that would not otherwise be normal, and so it can be a very positive experience if everyone thinks of it as a problem avoidance session.

Fig. 7.1 Example ranked risk log

ID	Description	Probability	Impact	Severity	Management action	Responsibilty
1	Integration test fail.	M	M	4	Insert technical review after module tests.	Project manager
2	Trader terminals unavailable for development work.	M	H	6	Buy two replica terminals for project.	John
3	User documentation not printed in time for roll-out.	M	M	4	Include .pdf version in online help.	Claire
4	Development system software upgrade not available.	L	L	1	Work with current version / monitor.	All

Either during the session or afterwards, go back through the list of risks and decide whether management actions other than acceptance are necessary, and identify appropriate actions. The most efficient way to do this is to sort the list of risks according to severity (see Fig. 7.1). Severity = probability × impact, with 1 point for low, 2 for medium and 3 for high. High impact, high probability risks (severity 9) almost certainly need some management action. Low probability, low impact risks (severity 1) almost certainly deserve nothing more than active acceptance of the risk – unless the management action is effectively free. Intermediate severity risks may require management action, depending on the cost-benefits of such action. Preventing higher severity risks usually justifies significant effort and expense; proportionately less effort can be justified if the risks can be reduced but not prevented. Remember that management action can include both specific actions aimed directly at the risk, and changes to the project plan to reduce or prevent the risk.

If you really cannot get people together for long enough to have a risk workshop, then work with an experienced colleague to draw up a basic list and then go and discuss this with experts from other areas in order to get enough different perspectives. Do not just e-mail a draft and ask for comments – this is a process that needs face-to-face interaction and creative stimulation.

▶ Continuous review

The risk workshop only provides the initial list of project risks. Some of the actions arising from the review can be built into the plan in the PID and others must wait until the project is under way. However, risk management is not a one-off exercise. It must be applied all the way through the project, and the list kept up to date as new information comes available. For example, the supplier failure that seemed very unlikely at the planning stage may begin to seem increasingly probable as the unanswered phone calls and e-mails begin to mount up, and the risk log should be updated accordingly.

Risk management is applied continually throughout the project in two ways: through periodic formal reviews, and through constant awareness of risk on the part of the project manager.

The periodic reviews can be specially organized events at critical points in the project and following the same format as the initial risk workshop. Alternatively, risks can be added to the agenda of all project meetings and other reviews, so that there is always a forum for emerging risks to be discussed and brought under control.

It is good practice to get into the habit of reserving a section on risks and recent discoveries in the regular project progress reports for the project sponsor. The section may be blank on many occasions, but putting this section in the report will make it much easier to raise risks and concerns when they appear.

At least as important as these formal mechanisms for managing risk is the project manager's constant awareness of risks. A large part of your time will be spent taking decisions about the project that involve a trade-off between time, cost and quality of deliverables. But all of these decisions also involve a risk dimension. Earlier in this book, the project manager's job was described in terms of a balancing act between cost, time and performance. But projects have four dimensions, not three (see Fig. 7.2). Risk is the fourth project dimension and it is possible to trade off any of the other dimensions against risk. Delivering the project faster, for less money, and with better deliverables might be possible, but it is bound to mean taking more risks and consequently accepting a lower probability of success. Where the firm is depending on a project – that is, the project's success is critical to the firm's success – the project must not be high risk. Such projects can therefore be long and expensive.

Fig. 7.2 Risk and project scope

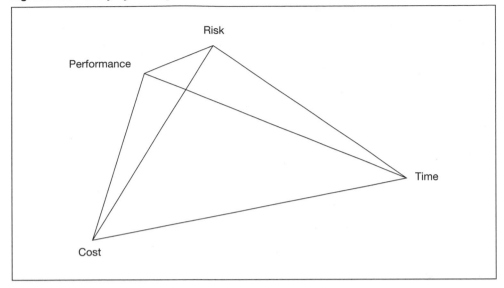

Part III
project life cycle stages

define

8

What is the define phase?

Objectives

Scope

Starting inputs

Deliverables

Responsibilities

Process

1
2
3
4
5
6
7
8
9
10
11

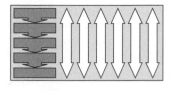

It should be self-evident that there has to be a clear decision point at which an organization can commit to a project. This decision point cannot, however, be the first thing that happens: the decision cannot be made without some basic information about the proposed project which must first be generated. So the most basic division of a project life cycle is between the initial planning and the work itself.

However, while some small projects are understood well enough for every aspect of the work to be planned from the outset, most projects initially involve some degree of uncertainty about their later stages. Rather than make an open-ended commitment to the project, the work is broken down into phases that correspond to the major steps from idea to implementation. This improves the quality of the information since there is less need to provide long distance forecasts, and it increases the flexibility to adapt plans to reflect changing circumstances.

As explained earlier, the phase breakdown described here is generally applicable to most projects but may need some common-sense adaptation for your circumstances. Such adaptation is likely to be minor, since the underlying requirements for many different sorts of activity are the same. Most projects should start with some thinking about the right approach followed by some work to address the basic questions. Later phases fill in the gaps and check that the result is sound. In rare cases, projects may simply not involve anything that corresponds to 'Test' or 'Implementation', and in these cases it would not make sense to force the projects to fit this framework exactly.

What is the define phase?

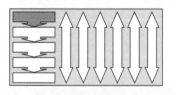

The define phase is the first package of project-related work. It is a group of activities directed towards agreeing what the project should attempt to achieve, deducing what will be involved in doing the project, and hence reaching a decision on whether the project is worth pursuing. We will assume that this process involves the creation and authorization of a project initiation document (PID).

All projects should be properly defined before any work starts. This should be self-evident, but it is surprising how many projects doom themselves to failure almost before they start, by failing to establish at the outset what needs to be done. Irrespective of the technical domain of your project, and however else its structure might differ from the generic life cycle described in this book, a define phase is always required.

Large projects may require weeks or even months of effort even to create a plan which adequately balances costs, timescales, risks and desired outputs. In this case, the define phase requires real resource allocations so that the team can devote themselves properly to their work, and it would be normal to authorize this use of resources as though it was itself a mini-project. So although the following phase description assumes that the define phase is a single block of work, on large projects there may be a preliminary 'initiate' phase that serves to describe exactly the define phase. The initiate phase follows the same structure as the define phase but rather than attempt to describe exactly the whole project its objective is only to describe the define phases (see Fig. 8.1).

Fig. 8.1 Small and large project define phases

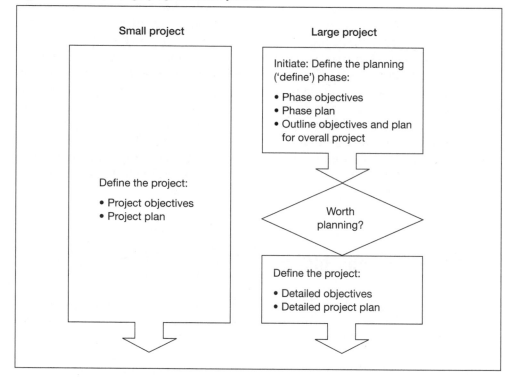

Objectives

The define phase objectives will usually include one or more of the following:

◆ Establish whether the proposal merits treatment as a project.
◆ Understand and document the initial user requirements and translate these into a format that can be used later to judge whether the project has finished.

- Identify the various stakeholders who would need to be involved, and build consensus among this group about the objectives and constraints of the proposed project.
- Clarify and quantify desired business benefits which should result from the project.
- Identify and note any known overlaps with the scope of other active or proposed projects. Depending on the status of the other projects, it may be appropriate to adapt the scope and plan of the currently proposed project.
- Carry out any preliminary studies or feasibility exercises that may be necessary to prove the best approach to use in the project.
- Plan the overall project in as much depth as possible, with clearly defined breakpoints if it is not possible to plan in detail through to completion. The plan must include timings, total costs (including quotes from subcontractors, if appropriate) and some reasonable assumptions about resource availability.
- Identify the project risks and assess which of these should be addressed in the plan.
- Summarize the above information in a PID that contains the initial business case.
- Gain approval for the project defined in the PID.

Scope

The define phase improves understanding of what the project will be – it should not involve doing any part of the project.

In scope	Out of scope
<ul><li>Talking to users and other stakeholders about what they want (or don't want) from the project.</li><li>Gathering information to quantify requirements and business benefits.</li><li>Clear thinking about limits of scope of the project.</li><li>Preliminary investigations to guide the choice of approaches.</li><li>Project planning, including risk analysis.</li><li>Preparing PID.</li></ul>	<ul><li>Solving users' immediate problems.</li><li>Planning beyond the detail necessary for task allocation.</li><li>Executing the project.</li></ul>

Starting inputs

Most organizations have a standard template for their equivalent of the PID.

The define phase is often set in motion by an engagement letter or other document, usually from the sponsor, which sets out the initial terms of reference.

Other necessary inputs for the define phase will vary from project to project – since this is the first phase, there are no inputs from earlier phases. Nonetheless, it will be very rare for there to be no other inputs at all, since this phase will usually involve gathering information from across the firm.

Deliverables

The deliverables at this stage consist of the following:

1 Completed Project Initiation Document (PID). This implies the following other deliverables:

   ◆ Detailed project plan, giving confidence in timings and costs of undertaking the project. This in turn may mean having completed a formal Request for Proposal/Supplier Selection exercise, and such feasibility studies as may be required to prove that the planned approach is valid.

   ◆ Risk assessment and management plan.

   ◆ 'Frozen' user requirements (not only must the requirements themselves be agreed and signed off by everyone concerned, but they must also agree that the requirements will not be changed thereafter without due process).

   ◆ Business case, showing how the project is justified by improved revenues, reduced costs or improved management of business risks.

2 Authorization for the project, in the form of an authorized PID.

Responsibilities

Idea originator

One of the heroes of the project process is the person who had the first idea for the project. This person must persuade others in the firm that the idea has enough value to merit at least an investigation into what the costs and benefits would be (a define phase study). This will involve, as a minimum, convincing a suitable sponsor to support the idea, but it may involve more discussions to refine the idea and build support before even this stage is reached.

In some cases, the idea originator may become the project manager. But often the idea originator will have to hand over the idea to a project manager. Then the two will have to work together during this phase to ensure that the project objectives and vision are completely understood.

▶ Sponsor

The sponsor's primary responsibility is to ensure that the proposed project provides the best balance of business benefits against invested money and resources. This involves:

◆ Setting aside sufficient time to understand the project and support the definition phase activities. This may involve taking part in negotiations with senior managers internally or externally in order to facilitate critical negotiations on behalf of the project.

◆ Reviewing and advising on aspects of the PID as it is in preparation, in order to ensure focus on business objectives.

◆ Signing off the completed PID so that it can be passed to the programme board for approval. (It is usual for sponsor approval to be separate from programme board approval. The sponsor's approval means 'I would support this project', whereas the board's approval means 'This project is the best of the currently available choices of the ways the firm can spend our resources, and we will therefore make those resources available.')

▶ Project manager

The project manager is responsible for:

◆ Ensuring their own understanding of the project objective.

◆ Defining the scope of the proposed project.

◆ If required during this phase: assembling, briefing and managing the define phase project team.

◆ Preparing the PID. This means:
  – negotiating and clarifying user requirements, scope, and objectives with interested parties, and recording the final agreements clearly and unambiguously;
  – producing the overall project plan, including timescales, costs and risk management plan.

▶ Programme board

The programme board will review the PID and compare the proposed project with other proposed uses of the company resources, and will either provide approval to proceed with the project, or will defer or reject the proposal. Approval of a PID by the board is usually approval to use the resources and spend the money specified in the PID.

▶ End-user representative

It is good practice to appoint someone to be the 'voice of the customer' for the project, though this may require some creativity if the end-users are external to the firm. This person has a decisive input into the final user requirements, and so they must be appointed at the define stage. Though the end-user representative should be part of the project team and should be committed to its success, it is important that they should also retain a degree of independence. The end-user representative's prime responsibility is to the customer, rather than to the project, and they should be able to distinguish between actions which help the project alone and actions which help the customer as well as the project.

The end-user representative will usually be an important signatory on the final user requirement documentation.

▶ External suppliers

Some projects rely on external suppliers for critical pieces of work. Whether this is the case will usually be clear at the definition stage. If an external supplier has an important role to play in the planned project, then they should be as involved in the planning as any comparable internal resource. The external supplier is responsible for:

◆ Ensuring and confirming their own understanding of the project objectives, and what their own role is to be in achieving those objectives.

◆ Providing timely and accurate responses to support the creation of a PID. This means co-operating with the task breakdown, allocation and estimating process, and participating fully in the risk identification and management activities.

▶ Process

▶ Initiate the project

The process starts with an idea that something needs to be done. Such ideas can come from anywhere in the organization, and it is important that they are not stifled. Powerful new concepts may sound outlandish at first simply because they do not fit with the accepted way of doing things – but this is precisely the sort of idea that most organizations need. Ideas should always be discussed with someone: bad ideas can always be filtered out later, but if good ideas are missed because nobody mentions them they are lost for ever.

It may be that the idea is something that one of the other parts of the firm is already set up to do, or that it can be done relatively quickly and with low risk without running it as a project. If this is the case, then it is not appropriate to treat the idea as a project.

Depending on the idea and the people involved, there may be some period of reflection and development, but the first real test comes when it is necessary to persuade a sponsor to support the idea. How this is done will depend on the people involved and the idea itself. Most sponsors will want some reason to believe that there will be real business benefits, and so the argument should contain the basis of a business case. However, if you are doing the work at this stage, do not invest more than minimal effort before the sponsor has joined the project, otherwise you will end up doing work without business backing. It is likely that the sponsor will

Fig. 8.2 Define phase process flowchart

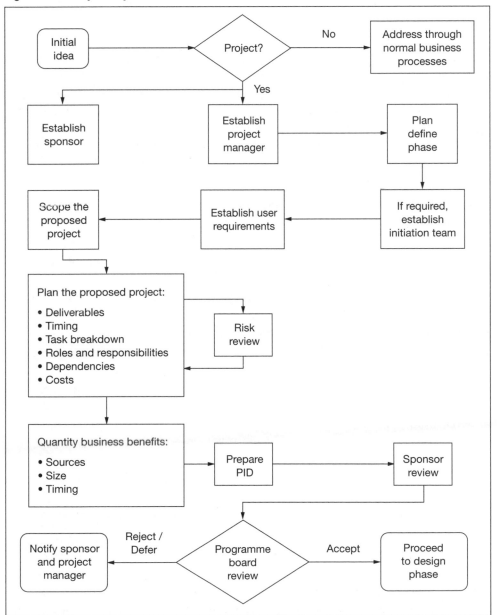

have many questions about the proposal at this early stage, but they should understand that the define phase exists precisely to find the answers to many of their questions.

In complex, multi-disciplinary projects, there may be a need to assemble a proposal team to work on the PID, in order to ensure adequate coverage of different parts of the business, technology areas, or geographic regions. The project manager will need to break down the work into tasks, allocate these to individuals, and co-ordinate work as with other phases of the project.

▶ Establish objectives and scope

The core activities of the phase are the scoping and planning of the overall project. Both depend on identifying the project objectives and the user requirements. For technical projects this process is formalized into the creation of a Requirements Specification, and some software engineering methods include formal ways to capture user requirements unambiguously. If your organization already has a procedure that can be re-applied to reduce project risk or simplify management tasks, it is good practice to do so. In general, the project objectives and user requirements together should describe the desired future state of the world once the project is finished. They should address:

◆ **Project deliverables:** what will they do? What inputs will they take, and what outputs will they produce? What has to happen in order to convert inputs to outputs?

◆ **System interfaces:** exactly how will the deliverable get its inputs and how will its outputs get to wherever they need to be?

◆ **System constraints:** are there any limitations on the time taken to do things, or the volume of material that can be handled, or the way that personal information can be stored, of which we need to be aware?

◆ **Roll-out:** is there a need to include particular features to aid the transition to the new solution? Are there any constraints on the sequence of roll-out locations?

◆ **User issues:** can we assume any technical or specialist knowledge from the end-users, and what does this mean for the project? Must we conform to certain user expectations about the appearance of the finished product? What languages will users be using?

◆ **Project constraints:** is there a critical deadline beyond which there is no point doing the project (a 'drop dead date')? Will we have access to the required hardware and people for the project? What is the cost of delay? What is the maximum number of people we could use? Are we approaching the capacity limit of our supplier?

◆ **Project dependencies:** does this project depend on another project to produce its output on time?

The scope of the project should be apparent once the user requirements are clear. Nonetheless, it is important to address scope as a separate issue because it prompts us to ask 'Now we know what the goal is, let's check to see what the goal is *not*.' This is the first part of project risk management, and experienced project managers know that an hour or two spent thinking carefully about scope at this stage can save many weekends later on. Experience also often brings a knack for spotting where the scope must be clearly limited in order to avoid confusion, but a good first step is to revisit every item on your list of initial user requirements and ask yourself a few basic questions:

1 Could somebody else reading this interpret it to mean much more work than I intended? If so, how do I clarify what I mean? For example:

 ◆ Do we really mean 'Market research interviews with customers', or do we mean 'Focus group interviews with nine groups of five customers at a time, to be conducted three at a time in South Africa, UK and US'?

 ◆ What do we mean by 'Find a solution to problem Z'? Do we mean 'Identify a range of solutions to problem Z and make a recommendation for the best', or do we mean 'Solve problem Z'? There is an important difference between identifying the solution and implementing it.

2 Are quantities and numbers given? Beware that different people have materially different understandings of words like 'some', 'enough' or 'reliable'.

3 Are there activities which we know must happen, but which we cannot undertake?

4 Are there any assumptions that need to be made about the availability of critical inputs? If so, why is it outside the scope of the project to procure those inputs?

Do not shy away from issues of uncertainty or disagreement at this stage. It may seem expedient to allow ambiguity so that everyone can believe that they will get what they want, but by doing so you are building in problems. Issues that seem expedient to avoid now will still need to be addressed later, but once this phase is complete you will have far less flexibility in dealing with them since you will be committed to a plan. Forcing a decision between incompatible requirements now may be uncomfortable, but it is much easier than trying to manage a project that has incompatible requirements built into its objectives.

eg

Personal attack alarm

A project team was charged with designing a personal attack alarm for women. They interviewed a range of women and confirmed that fear of attack was a common theme, and that whatever was designed would have to fit into a handbag. But the team did not feel that they really understood the core of what the women wanted from an attack alarm, and their interview subjects gave a wide range of contradictory answers when asked to imagine what their ideal device would be. So the team made a range of models, each embodying different design features: some were simple shapes, some were shaped like weapons, and others were ergonomically sculpted to fit in the hand. One model was almost left out of the set because the team felt that its long thin form was too suggestive and would be offensive to women, but to the surprise of the team this was the model that was the clear ▶

favourite in subsequent interviews. Questioning revealed that there was another common deep-seated fear alongside the fear of attack, and that was the fear of humiliation. Many women were ashamed that they were considering buying an attack alarm, and they certainly did not want anything in their handbag that looked like an attack alarm, in case their friends or colleagues caught sight of it. What the design team had thought would be far too suggestive had only one meaning for the women: it looked like a tube of make-up. So the women could carry it in their handbags without shame.

The team would never have discovered what actually lay behind the decision to buy (or not to buy) an attack alarm if they had not given their interviewees a sufficient range of models that allowed them to describe the different versions in their own terms, and thereby reveal their true preferences. The users could not initially describe their ideal solution, but neither could the design team.

!

Common sense

This early stage is the best time to pre-empt any possible misunderstanding about objectives. This means taking extra care during conversations with stakeholders. When discussing user requirements it is easy to believe that the person you are talking to shares your understanding of the intended outputs, whereas they may have a good understanding, but one which is different from yours. Avoid this by asking open questions, and by inviting the other person to explain what they would expect to see as a project output in their own words (instead of 'Do you understand?', ask 'Could you tell me what you think the finished X will look like?').

▶ Plan the project

To a certain extent, planning, establishing user requirements, and scoping proceed hand in hand. By the time the scope and user requirements are clear, you should already have a good idea about the blocks of work that will be required. The process of generating a project plan is covered in more depth earlier in this book, so there is no need to spend more time on it here. The plan should cover the whole project (unless the define phase is split, as described earlier for a large project) and should include:

- Roles and responsibilities for individuals with the best information available at the time regarding their availability.
- Known dependencies within and outside the project.
- Risks and planned management actions, including any explicit contingency plans with their associated funding and resource needs.
- Predicted spending and resource usage profile during the project.

▶ Project business case

Businesses invest money, time and resources in projects in the hope that the benefits will outweigh the costs. This balance between costs and benefits is summarized in the project business case. Direct project costs should be known from the project plan, but the benefits will come from the changes in the business that the project is intended to bring about. Despite the wide range of possible projects it should always be possible to trace the business benefits back to one or more of the following:

1 **Increasing revenues.** For example, increasing sales, or launching a new product line, or entering a new market.

2 **Decreasing costs.** For example, lower materials usage, switching to cheaper assembly methods, or increasing throughput.

3 **Decreasing capital requirements.** Capital is money tied up in things the business owns but does not sell immediately (e.g. plant and equipment, or stock). Projects to decrease capital requirements aim to let the firm do more with less. For example, restructuring the firm's supply chain to improve responsiveness to the market can also have dramatic benefits for the amount of money tied up in stock.

4 **Meet a legal or regulatory requirement.** Note that value can still be created on such projects if you run your project well and it costs your firm less to meet the requirement than your competitors.

5 **Reduce business risk.** Businesses have risks, just like projects. These range from large single events to everyday variability in processes, and they contribute to uncertainty in future costs and revenues. The value of avoiding individual risks can be calculated by assessing probabilities and costs quantitatively.

Your organization may recognize many other types of benefits, but you should always seek to link any claimed benefit back to one or more of the above categories. If there is not even an indirect link, then the project probably does not have any real business benefits. In particular, beware of anyone claiming vague 'strategic' benefits unless they are supported by an explanation of how the strategy will influence the five core business benefit categories.

Many companies have found, however, that there are some non-financial parameters that are useful diagnostics for the business and these companies will often justify projects on the basis of improvements in these parameters. Whether this is wise for your particular project depends on whether the project is aimed at improving the business process that the parameter measures, or whether the project is aimed at the parameter alone (hence it is just gaming the measurement system). Well-chosen non-financial metrics such as customer satisfaction ratings or process quality metrics can be useful because they are measurable today but give a prediction of how the hard business numbers will change tomorrow. If the company management uses such parameters explicitly to measure overall company performance in a balanced scorecard, then it can be useful to link project benefits back to these parameters.

Of course, the most compelling business argument for your project will be if you demonstrate that the benefits outweigh the costs using hard numbers. To do this you need to be able to quantify the project's impact on costs, revenues, capital usage and so on. You do not usually to have construct a model of the whole company finances before and after the project since the benefit comes from the change. Calculating the increase in revenues or decrease in costs is fine.

When calculating the financial impact of a project it is necessary to construct a model that shows how the project will create the business benefits (usually extra money). If your project has an output that is sold in the market then it is clear that the extra money comes from the additional profit. Similarly if your project aims to cut external spending then this is relatively easy to quantify. But many projects are internal and do not have such a direct relationship to company costs and revenues. In most organizations there are standard costs for various standard activities, and you may be able to use these if your project aims to modify how much of each activity gets done. If your project will change the way that things are done significantly, or change the way that resources are used in different departments, you should probably consult your firm's management accounting department for advice on how to get a true picture of the likely impact of the project.

The benefits that result from a project are likely to be spread over time. The project may result in a step change in business costs or revenues that happens on the day the project finishes, and continues indefinitely. It is more likely that there will be some delay before benefits can be felt and the benefits will then grow for some period before falling away as the business moves further ahead. This sort of profile for projected benefits can change the attractiveness of a project, and for big projects it is worthwhile investing significant effort in making a proper assessment of when the benefits are likely to be felt. Optimistic or pessimistic assumptions about the size or the timing of benefits can lead to poor investment decisions and so you should always try to remain neutral when making such projections.

Presenting a projection of the profile of anticipated business benefits can be very informative, but it is difficult to compare the attractiveness of competing projects with different profiles. Business managers use several recognized techniques for summarizing and quantifying the relative benefits of projects in a consistent way. These are breakeven analysis, net present value (NPV) and internal rate of return (IRR).

▶ Breakeven

The simplest measure of financial attractiveness is the project breakeven time. This is the measure of how long from the start of the project it takes for the project costs to be paid back by the project benefits. So in Fig. 8.3, a project with a required investment of £1,000 is done during year 0, and in each subsequent year there are benefits of £250. So the payback time is four years.

Calculating payback time is usually quite easy. If you cannot manage the maths needed to work out the payback time directly, plot the net cash position on a graph and read off the time when the line crosses the cash axis from negative to positive.

Projects with a short payback time are usually more attractive than those with a long payback time, and some companies apply a simple threshold of a maximum payback time (often three years). But doing this means that the company will reject an investment opportunity that pays back after three years even if the ultimate payoff is very large, and if everyone followed this policy then nobody would ever undertake large construction projects or other long-term investments. Simple payback only looks at the time to pay back the project investment; it provides no means to distinguish between investments that have different pay-offs. Furthermore, simple payback calculations do not take into account the fact that money tied up in the project could have been invested elsewhere in the firm where it would have earned the firm's normal rate of return. These weaknesses are overcome by looking at a project's net present value or internal rate of return.

Fig. 8.3 Simple payback

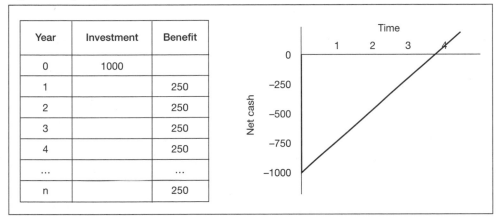

▶ Net present value

The key to this concept is discounting or 'time value of money'. If you borrow £100 today at 10% interest to be paid back in exactly one year, the future payment will be £110. Having £100 today means the same thing as having £110 in one year's time. Put another way, £110 one year from now has a present value of £100 at a discount rate of 10%. For those unfamiliar with the concept it may seem strange that a pound today is not worth a pound in the future, but this is a direct consequence of paying interest. We could apply the same logic in reverse to calculate how much we would need to invest today in order to have £100 in one year:

At an interest rate r of 10% (0.10) our investment c would become £100 in one year:

$$c(1 + 0.10) = 100$$

$$c = \frac{100}{1.10} = 90.91$$

Applying this to the project investment decision gives a very useful decision-making guide. If you had to choose whether to invest £100 in a project today with the promise that it would create a pay-off of £100 in one year, you would be better off if you ignored the project and put your money in the bank instead. The project would be an attractive investment if its promised pay-off at the end of the year was more than £110, since the present value of any amount over £110 would be more than the £100 you would need to invest today.

The same logic would apply if the pay-off came in two parts, one £60 a year from now, and a second £60 payment one year later. In this case the present value of the pay-offs is the present value of £60 discounted for one year plus the present value of the other £60 discounted for two years.

The present value of £60 that you will receive in one year is:

$$\frac{60}{1 + 0.10} = 54.54$$

To find the present value of the second payment it must be discounted twice since it will not appear for two years. So its present value is:

$$60 \times \frac{1}{1 + 0.10} \times \frac{1}{1 + 0.10} = \frac{60}{1.10^2} = 49.59$$

The project is an attractive investment if the present value of the pay-offs is greater than the present value of the investment. Subtracting the initial project investment (–£100) from the two pay-off present values (£54.54 + £49.59) leaves a net present value for the overall project of £4.13. So the project is still attractive.

Time	0	1	2
Investment	−100		
Pay-off		+60	+60
Discount rate	0.10	0.10	0.10
Discount factor	1	1/1.10	1/1.10²
Present value	−100	+54.54	+49.59

	Net present value	+4.13

By working with colleagues who have access to relevant numbers you should be able to draw up a table showing the predicted size and timing of project costs and benefits. The table should show cash spending and income in each month or year as far into the future as you can predict. Benefits will always fade away eventually so you should not assume that benefits will continue for ever. For each period in the future, calculate the present value of the cash flow by applying a discount factor compounded by the number of periods into the future. So if the discount rate is r, and cash flow c occurs n periods into the future, then the present value of the cash flow is:

$$PV(c) = c \, \frac{1}{(1 + r)^n}$$

Remember that cash you spend on the project is negative and extra cash coming into the firm is positive. So you can sum the present values of all the positive and negative cash flows in all the periods to a single number: the net present value. If the net present value is negative, then the money would be better invested elsewhere in the firm and the project should not be pursued. Though a large positive NPV is better than a small one, do not assume that an NPV of zero indicates that there is no profit in the project, since the discount rate used to calculate the NPV already allows for the company's usual profits.

But what is an appropriate discount rate to use in these calculations? In order to pay for your project, your organization must use some of the money that has been lent to it by banks and other investors. These organizations make investments in firms because they expect to make good returns on these investments. If your competitors offer a better rate of return than you, then (all other things being equal) investors will put their money into your competitors. So your firm's external investors require a rate of return that is set partly by the characteristics of your firm and partly by the other choices available to them. This required rate of return is called the firm's cost of capital, and all the activities that the firm undertakes, including projects, should each have a financial rate of return above the firm's cost of capital. The appropriate rate to apply in NPV calculations, therefore, is the firm's cost of capital. (Finance purists may insist that the appropriate rate is one that treats each project as a separate business, rather than the aggregate rate for the whole company. This has some theoretical merit but it can only be applied in practice on rare projects that are large enough to have the characteristics of a separate company.)

If you are using a spreadsheet package, net present value is no harder to calculate than payback time, but it is a much more powerful guide to the attractiveness of an investment. It allows short- and long-term investments to be compared on an equal basis, and can even handle projects with unusual cash-flow profiles without difficulty.

▶ IRR and hurdle rates

Many organizations define a minimum rate of return on their project investments known as the hurdle rate. This is no lower than the firm's cost of capital, but may be slightly higher if the firm has a wide choice of available projects and wishes to filter out all but the best, or it wishes to minimize the chance that an estimating error will allow a project with actual returns below the cost of capital to slip through.

The internal rate of return on an investment is the discount rate that sets the net present value to zero. To calculate IRR, set up a cash-flow projection spreadsheet as for calculating NPV, but make the discount rate r a variable. Then, either by trial and error, or using the automatic solution-finding tool in your spreadsheet, find the value of r that sets the project NPV to zero.

In many cases saying that a project has an IRR above the cost of capital and saying that it has a positive NPV are exactly equivalent. But IRR does have drawbacks. It has problems if the net cash position of the project changes between positive and negative more than once during the life of the investment. Furthermore, it does not provide information on the absolute size of the potential benefits. So a firm faced with a choice between two projects each with an IRR of 21%, may not know which to choose, despite the fact that one project promised 21% return on an investment of £10,000, whereas the other promised the same return on an investment of £100,000. Despite these weaknesses, IRRs and hurdle rates are the most common way to assess the likely return on a project investment.

▶ Sensitivity

Do not get carried away with the cash-flow projections in your spreadsheets. Everyone knows that they are only an estimate. What will reassure people reading your business case is if you can show that the project is still viable even if your estimate turns out to be wrong. So revisit your numbers and explore what would happen if the project took longer to complete than planned, or cost significantly more, or the benefits proved elusive. Any project that is only viable if none of the starting assumptions changes by more than a small amount is probably just too dangerous to pursue, even if it looks attractive in the base case. If the project is attractive with a discount rate of 12.0% but becomes unattractive when the discount rate climbs to 12.2% then it is at best a marginal investment.

It is often useful to calculate how much of a change in key parameters would be required to destroy the attractiveness of the project, since this will tell you useful information about the project constraints. It is extremely helpful for the project manager to know that, for example, a 5% time overrun will make the project unattractive but that it would require a 27% cost overrun to achieve the same result.

▶ Create project initiation document (PID)

With a good understanding of the user requirements, the plan and the business justification, you should have all the information needed to create a PID with very little extra work. This is supposed to be the document that defines the project. Read it through carefully yourself after drafting it, paying particular attention to words which are ambiguous or which rely on assumptions or other information for their correct interpretation. It is intended to be a standalone document and any clarification, definition, or necessary background should be included either directly or in a reference.

Review the draft PID with your project sponsor, who will ensure that it contains the necessary information, and who may also ask for clarification if some points are unclear. In order to minimize the amount of rework required, it is a good idea to keep the sponsor fully briefed on the information which will appear in the PID as it comes available so that there are no surprises once the whole document appears. It is possible that what looked attractive initially is less attractive once all the facts discovered during this phase of work are taken into account. If this happens, then either the exercise can be halted (with a sigh of relief that not too much time was spent on it), or the scope or objectives can be adjusted in some way that avoids the problems.

Once the project sponsor has approved the PID, it is passed to the programme board. The programme board usually meets regularly and will review each PID submitted during a period for business costs and benefits, and will also compare them against each other and ongoing projects. The board can either accept a PID, defer it, or reject it.

When a PID is accepted by the board this is authorization to proceed with the design phase.

eg

West Coast Main Line upgrade

The West Coast Main Line is one of the most important trunk routes in Britain's rail network, but after many years of under-investment its status in the late 1990s was critical. A modernization programme costing £2.1 billion was announced in 1998. This would not only refurbish the line but also upgrade it to increase its capacity and allow trains to run safely at up to 225 km/h (140mph) – and one of the train operating companies invested in a fleet of 53 high-speed trains to take advantage of this capability.

By 2002, the cost of the programme had risen to almost £10 billion, and would have risen far higher had many of the upgrade features that formed part of the original project justification not been abandoned. The train operator received £100 million compensation from the company responsible for the project to cover the losses arising from the disruption to their services and the incremental cost of a fleet of high-speed trains that would now, in fact, only be able to run at the same speed as other trains.

The project was large and complex and the problems were the compounded result of many factors. But underlying many of them was a lack of rigour in the define phase. For example:

- The planned upgrade to 225 km/h operation relied on a new unproven signalling technology, but whatever risk analysis was undertaken did not identify that this was an 'unacceptable risk' until after contracts had been signed committing the railway company to providing high-speed capability. A later risk analysis did identify this risk and the new signalling technology was abandoned – but only after the high-speed trains had been bought!

- The project budget and plan were created without reference to a valid track asset register, and so there was no way that the planners could have known what the company owned, let alone what its current status was and what would be involved in upgrading it. Furthermore, engineering audits that might have helped to get a clear picture of what was involved in some areas were scrapped.

- Exact specifications for enhancements were not agreed with contractors at the outset, and the scope of many sub-projects had yet to be determined in June 2002, though planning had started in 1994.

Pulling together enough information to be able to define the project properly at the outset would have involved more time and effort than was actually spent during the define phase. But the pay-off in terms of avoided wastage later on would have been great.

? Ten key questions: preliminary definition

1 Do you have an unambiguous understanding of what the end-users would like and why? If there are different user groups, do you know how their wants differ?   Yes/No

2 Do you understand users' priorities for performance, timing and cost?

3 Do you have an outline project plan that will give deliverables with adequate performance, fast enough, and cheaply enough?   Yes/No

4 Have you identified the basic questions that must be answered before we know enough to say whether the project is viable?   Yes/No

5 Does the project have a sponsor – a senior manager who will champion the proposal and underwrite the costs of this phase?   Yes/No

6 Do you have a draft business case for the project explaining the anticipated business benefits and giving a broad range of project costs?   Yes/No

7 Can you describe the scope of the project? (What is included and what not? At what stage will the project outputs become somebody else's responsibility?)   Yes/No

8 Can you describe in broad terms who (individuals or organizations) will do each of the major blocks of work through to the end of the project?   Yes/No

9 Do you have a plan for the rest of the define phase in sufficient detail for task allocation?   Yes/No

10 Does the programme board (the senior managers who allocate funds and resources to projects) consider that the project is sufficiently attractive in its own right and in relation to other business needs to justify investment in the define phase?   Yes/No

Ten key questions: full definition

1 Do you have a realistic plan (see Planning questions) that covers the whole project in sufficient depth to allow task allocation? **Yes/No**

2 Are user requirements (including not only what the outputs should be, but how they will be delivered and what user involvement is expected) agreed and frozen? Are these documented in a form that can be used later to assess whether the project has delivered successfully? **Yes/No**

3 Does the plan assume only proven technology and procedures? If not, have preliminary proof-of-concept investigations shown that the proposed approach is viable? **Yes/No**

4 Does the business case include all the costs of doing the project (including all expenditures, a realistic cost of people's time, and allowance for any revenues that would have to be foregone)? **Yes/No**

5 Does the business case include a realistic assessment of the size and likely timing of business benefits arising from the project? **Yes/No**

6 Are assumptions about factors that might influence costs and benefits stated clearly, and have you considered what might happen if any of these change slightly? **Yes/No**

7 Does the project support the stated strategic objectives of the company? **Yes/No**

8 Does the management of the firm believe that this project represents the best use of money and resources (e.g. when compared with other possible projects)? **Yes/No**

9 Have the management group explicitly authorized the project, and will they ensure that the necessary money, resources and management support are available for it? **Yes/No**

10 Would you be confident that someone who has not been involved in the project could read your PID and would then be able to manage the project through to the arrival of the desired business benefits? **Yes/No**

design

1
2
3
4
5
6
7
8
9
10
11

What is the design phase?

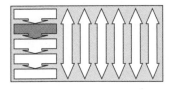

The design phase is where we create the solution that we hope will match the user requirements which were agreed during project definition. We will receive confirmation that this goal has been achieved during the later test phase. Depending on the nature of the work there may also be a separate build phase, but on software projects, for example, the design and build phase are synonymous. You should adapt your project structure to suit the needs of the project, increasing or reducing the importance of the phases as necessary. Beware of reducing the number of phases too far: it is important to have some logical structure so that different sorts of work do not clash with each other and we go into each phase with a clear plan that will take us through to its end. Conversely, forcing a project into too many phases which do not fit naturally with the major blocks of work disrupts the project without reducing risk.

The design phase of a project is where the first substantial technical work gets done. Note, however, that it is only the first technical work: it is usual to separate the design work from building, testing and roll-out, so as to minimize rework and disruption which would arise from testing partially-designed solutions or rolling out partially-tested systems. Non-technical projects usually also need a phase analogous to the design phase. For example, on market research projects, the interview guides and respondent selection guidelines might need to be set up carefully with reference to the statistical profile of the market – in other words, the research programme needs to be designed.

Objectives

The objectives of the design phase are to:

◆ generate a design for the solution that will satisfy the user requirements;

◆ create a test strategy that will reveal areas of the solution which do not meet user requirements, and that can subsequently show that the redesigned solution does meet the full user requirements;

◆ produce an updated and re-confirmed plan for the test phase of the project;

◆ manage the phase according to the plan set out in the PID, leading to phase completion on time, at the agreed cost, and with acceptable risk.

▶ Scope

In scope	Out of scope

◆ Technical work to interpret the specific user requirements and the general firm-wide requirements, and:
 	
  – create an overall technical approach or architecture that will satisfy the requirements in a coherent way;
 	
  – generate detailed implementations of each part of the architecture so that the whole solution is created.
 	
◆ Discussions with users about detailed questions to ensure exact fit with requirements.
	◆ Any activity not explicitly included in the plan! (Requested changes should be handled through the scope management process.)
	
	◆ Integrated testing of the whole solution.
	
	◆ Rolling out the solution to users other than as part of some pre-arranged user panel to help development.

▶ Starting inputs

The minimum inputs that should be available are:

◆ Signed, authorized Product Initiation Document (PID) with concomitant funding and resources.

◆ Agreed user requirements.

◆ Firm-wide constraints or procedures that will influence the solution. (For example, this could include quality standards, corporate branding guidelines for material for publication, software engineering standards that must be followed, or constraints from the need for compatibility with pre-existing systems.)

▶ Deliverables

The following deliverables are required:

◆ A solution that can be shown to address each and every part of the user requirements. (Note that addressing a requirement in this sense does not mean being able to prove definitively that the requirement is met. It simply means that every requirement corresponds to some feature of the finished design. The proof will follow during the test phase.)

◆ A re-confirmed plan for the subsequent phases incorporating the effects of all the new information discovered during the design phase.

◆ Regular project progress and status reports for the sponsor and programme board.

Responsibilities

▶ Sponsor

The sponsor is responsible for ensuring that the funds and resources allocated to the project are well spent and are kept in line with the anticipated business objectives. The sponsor's involvement will vary depending on the experience of the project manager and the scale and status of the project.

As a minimum the sponsor's responsibility is to monitor progress against plan as reported in the weekly reports from the project manager, and to intervene to protect the project investment if required.

The sponsor will sometimes also take on the role of a senior ambassador for the project, building support among other senior staff in anticipation of the project deliverables, so that they will be greeted enthusiastically. Similarly, the sponsor may need to become involved in negotiations on behalf of the project with other groups inside or outside the firm.

▶ Project manager

The project manager is responsible for:

◆ Assembling the project team and allocating task responsibility and authority to team members unambiguously so that each can pursue their allocated tasks independently.

◆ Monitoring progress against plan and managing the critical chain.

A project manager's work includes management of the project, but sometimes it can also include non-management project work of the kind undertaken by other members of the team. When a project manager is doing both these types of work, it is vital for them to distinguish between the two types of work. If you are a project manager and you have also allocated yourself technical tasks on the project, then you need to split yourself in two, so that the technical part has team member responsibilities and works for the managing part. This is a normal way of working on small and medium-sized projects, but it is important that the project manager follows the same rules as everyone else when acting in their capacity as technical team member.

▶ Team members

Team members should:

◆ Ensure that they have a clear and correct understanding of the tasks they have been asked to do. This involves not only clarifying the technical nature of their personal deliverables, but also clarifying what inputs to use, what to do with the deliverables once they are created, and when the deliverables should be produced.

◆ Use their skill and initiative to execute the tasks assigned by the project manager, taking responsibility and authority within the agreed boundaries for each task.

◆ Report progress, problems and concerns in good time to the project manager. This may mean raising issues actively rather than waiting until asked.

◆ Acknowledge that responsibility for project success is held jointly by the project team, which means that team members should support each other actively rather than have each individual working only for their own benefit.

▶ Programme board

The programme board will:

◆ Intervene to take corrective action on projects on an exception basis, using the information provided in the project status reports.

◆ When necessary, change the prioritization of the projects in the firm's portfolio to reflect new information. This may mean that existing projects are upgraded, and have better access to resources, but it may also mean that existing projects are downgraded. If this happens, then the affected project may lose resources with obvious schedule implications.

▶ End-user representative

The end-user representative has one clear responsibility: to bring the voice of the end-user into the heart of the project work. There is an obvious way for this to happen during the define phase through the process of defining user requirements, but it is important that the people working on the project are not allowed to forget the end-user once the technical work starts. How this is done will depend on the project, but it might include involvement in reviews, inclusion in circulation lists, and walk-throughs of work so far.

▶ External suppliers

To a large extent, suppliers should take on the responsibilities of team members. Project managers should make these expectations clear during initial negotiations and should also ensure that there are no clashes between these requirements and the contractual terms.

▶ Process

The programme board's approval of the PID launches a project. The project manager then has the authority to call on resources and spend funds up to the limits set out in the PID. With this authorization the project manager can revisit the project plan and update it to reflect actual resource availability and the assigned project priority. Resources can now be booked in the knowledge of their actual

Fig. 9.1 Design phase process flowchart

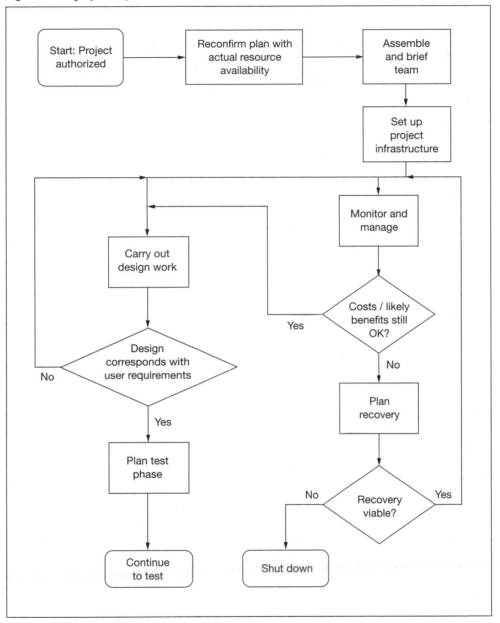

commitments on other activities, including their work on other projects that may have higher or lower priorities. Though the plan in the PID should have made reasonable assumptions about resource availability, it is quite possible that the situation will have changed by the time the project is authorized, particularly if it has been deferred for a while, and so the project timeline may be longer or shorter than the original plan. This is a natural consequence of the process of project selection and does not mean that projects whose timing stretches this way are somehow late – but it does mean that the project manager must communicate the revised timing to the interested parties as soon as possible.

The re-planning process involves assigning people to work on the project. If the company IT system supports it this might be done partly online, but it will usually involve some direct negotiation with the people involved and their line managers. Where there is a resource database everyone should make sure that the information in it is up to date, but a quick phone call is worthwhile to avoid the aggravation involved in re-planning a project because somebody appeared to be available but wasn't.

Line managers will often only commit to provide unnamed resources before the PID is authorized, so that they retain as much control as possible over their own team. This is reasonable, but it poses a problem for you, the project manager: you may not be able to predict whether the person you will get will be highly skilled and able to operate independently, or inexperienced and requiring constant supervision. Finding out you have been assigned the latter when you had planned around having the former can confound your plans at an early stage. The solution is to make sure that the line manager knows exactly what your project staffing requirements are. If you ask for 'someone from your group', you are saying that anyone who is available will do. Compare this with: 'This task is on the critical chain and is central to the project. It requires advanced skills in XYZ that I don't have and wouldn't know how to supervise, so I will have to be able to rely on this person to deliver promptly without relying on me for support.' This still allows the line manager freedom to decide who to allocate, but it provides more information about the sort of person needed. You always have the option of asking for named individuals, but remember that good people are probably in high demand, and so you may be in a queue.

As a last check once the team is known, it is worthwhile re-checking with the individuals concerned whether they have other commitments on their time. People often have holiday plans that do not appear in the database until the holiday is booked, or they may be aware of other factors that will affect their availability. Build all of this information into the plan before re-issuing it or, in emergencies, go and find replacements!

Each member of the team needs to be briefed not only about their tasks but also about what the project is for, how the project team will be organized and what administrative procedures will be followed. The most efficient way to do this is in a kick-off meeting, with the whole project team present (see Fig. 9.2) so that everyone hears the same message and people understand not only their own task, but also other people's tasks.

One of the first tasks is usually to set up the project infrastructure. Some projects can run without any special infrastructure other than a central project file for document storage. Others cannot work at all without a specific project office set up for the project, where team members can work together and concentrate on the project without fear of being overhead, or where key suppliers can have a desk without having access to other parts of the firm. There may be a need for special hardware, or dedicated links which must be set up with outside organizations. All of this should have been identified in the project plan, and time and money set aside for the work involved.

> ### Common sense
>
> On large, long projects with complex reporting structures, it is sometimes necessary to issue a written task description to each team member, specifying the scope and inputs and outputs of the task exactly. This is because written task descriptions, derived directly from the plan, are the only way to ensure that the scopes of all the tasks cover everything that has to be done with no gaps and no overlaps. On small projects, a project manager can check that everyone's activities fit together properly by having conversations with the people involved, but on large projects this is impractical.

Fig. 9.2 Draft kick-off meeting agenda

Introduction	Overview of the project origins and business objectives.
Team	Who is in the team; who is responsible for what area; what is the reporting structure if there are sub-teams; who are the other people we need to deal with (stakeholders, suppliers etc).
Plan outline	Overview of the project phases, with summary of phase deliverables and timing.
Immediate tasks	Activities that have to start this week explained in detail. Allocate each to named team members and get acknowledgement that they understand the task, that they know where to find their starting inputs, and that they can start immediately.
Administration	Contact details, where the full-time members will be based, how and where we will store documents and control versions; how and when people should report progress; technical or project control procedures to be observed; signatory and purchase limits etc.

With a fully briefed team working in a suitable environment, the design work can start. From the project manager's viewpoint this means that people will work on tasks, hand over task deliverables, and move on to other tasks. The project manager should apply all of the project management processes described earlier in this book, tracking and reporting progress, managing the critical chain, balancing performance, timescale, cost and risk, and communicating with the team and the sponsor. The phase ends when all the deliverables are available in a format that indicates that all the user requirements will be met. Conceptually, this might be done by waiting until all the deliverables are available and then reviewing them all against the list of user requirements, but this would be very inefficient and it is not what happens. In practice, the project manager should have a good idea of the extent to which the current output meets requirements at any time through the project. This way, corrective action can be taken immediately rather than waiting for the end of the phase to discover something is wrong. There is usually an end-of-phase review, which may incorporate a technical review, but the purpose of this should be to provide independent confirmation of the design, and project managers do not usually hold such a review without appropriate grounds to believe that the project will pass.

The build and test phase, which follows after the design phase, can sometimes only be planned in outline until the design is complete, since the arrangement of building and testing activities depends on the design. So once there is confirmation that the design is complete, there is enough information to re-issue the project plan with updated information. This provides a last checkpoint in the design phase to re-confirm that the project is still commercially attractive, before proceeding with testing.

Despite the best efforts of project managers, projects sometimes go astray. The project leader should recognize the danger signs and take prompt appropriate action, as described under 'Monitoring and control' in Chapter 6.

Most of the recovery actions will involve updating the plan, first so that we know what the true probable schedule is if no action is taken, and second to show the effect of any corrective action. It is possible that re-planning the project will show that the business objectives are much further away than originally believed, particularly if there is a hard 'drop dead date' external deadline which seems likely to be missed. If this is the case then the correct thing to do is to examine ways to bring the target and the project back in line, and, if no way can be found, to stop the project. The organization will be better off if projects that no longer make business sense are stopped. This may be uncomfortable for a project manager to do, but your organization would far prefer to be told early enough to stop wasting further money and resources. In practice, the project manager will rarely be left alone to take this decision. The project sponsor and the user group will become involved as soon as it becomes clear that the objectives are under threat and will participate in deciding what action to take. The programme board monitors projects for progress against plan and will call for corrective action if necessary. The board will need to re-approve an updated plan or PID which includes changes to the objectives, timescales, resource needs or costs, and rejection of such a recovery plan usually means that the project is cancelled unless further recovery actions can be planned.

Ten key questions: design

1. Did the phase start with explicit authorization to proceed with the project defined in the PDD, including authorization to spend money and acknowledgement of risks with their proposed management actions? Yes/No

2. Are you sure that the user requirements agreed during the definition phase are still acceptable? Are you sure that no other requirements or constraints have been added (i.e. are you managing scope creep)? Yes/No

3. Does the proposed project output (design) embody features that should satisfy all of the user requirements? If not, do you have agreement from the users that this change is acceptable? Yes/No

4. Is the plan proving to be broadly representative of what actually happens? If not, can you identify what is causing the problems and either remove the obstacle or re-issue the plan to reflect reality? Yes/No

5. Is the team working together as a team? Is there timely and open communication? Yes/No

6. Has the project been getting the resources and management support promised when authorization was given? Yes/No

7. Do you always know where the project stands against the plan? (Do team members keep you informed of progress?) Yes/No

8. Is the plan always up to date, including not only actual progress and prognosis information, but also new information about risks and other changes as they emerge? Yes/No

9. Are the anticipated project costs and timings acceptable to the users? Yes/No

10. Using the best information available at the end of the phase, can you say that the anticipated business benefits outweigh the remaining costs? Yes/No

build and test

What is the build and test phase?

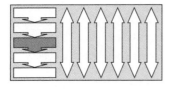 If the project involves creating new hardware of some kind (a product, a piece of manufacturing equipment, a building and so on) then the hardware is built during the build phase. It is built to the design that was approved in the end-of-phase review conducted at the end of the design phase. On projects to produce one-off items such as a bridge, whatever is built during the build phase will be handed over to the end-users. On projects to create a new product, however, what is created during the build phase will be a series of prototypes progressing towards the final production version of the product. On either sort of project there may also be manufacturing equipment produced as well as test articles to prove various aspects of the design.

Though building and testing are conceptually separate activities, it is usual to overlap the two to some extent. Individual parts are tested and validated before they are built into sub-systems, and there are tested and validated before they are assembled into the complete design. This approach has been shown to be the best way to isolate technical risks and reduce the time taken to discover problems. In some cases there may have been some test equipment built and tested during the design phase or even the define phase in order to provide evidence that the proposed approach was valid. So some organizations condense design, build and test into a single 'develop' phase. Your organization may work with more or fewer phases but whatever the split, the project output needs to be tested so that all the issues can be resolved before it is handed over to users. Well-designed technology often embodies features to make testing faster and more likely to pick up all the problems, but some amount of testing is always required.

Non-technology projects also benefit from testing, though it takes a different form. Experience has taught technology developers the necessity of testing, but projects in other disciplines would often benefit from the same approach. A dry run of a process, or a limited trial, can tell us what is likely to happen in the real world. These lessons are better learned in a safe setting and corrections made *before* our public reputation is put on the line. Some people distinguish between tests, which are internal within the organization, and trials, which happen in a less controlled public environment. Using this distinction, it should be clear that trials should follow internal tests.

Objectives

The objective of this phase is to demonstrate that the project output fulfils the user requirements set out in the project definition phase. This usually implies a subsidiary objective of building one or more complete sets of project outputs and refining these so that they pass the necessary tests reliably.

Scope

In scope	Out of scope
◆ Building one or more examples of the design up to the limits set out in the plan/. ◆ Design, build and validation of equipment to manufacture the design if appropriate. ◆ Preparation and approval of test procedures. ◆ Creation and validation of such test hardware and software as may be required. ◆ Testing of the designed solution in parts and as a whole to establish whether user requirements are met. ◆ Remedial action to correct non-compliance.	◆ Resolving differences between what users say they want now and what they said during project definition (use the scope management process!). ◆ Supporting any use of the project outputs outside agreed tests.

Starting inputs

The following inputs should be available:

◆ PID authorized by the programme steering committee.

◆ User requirements (may be incorporated in PID).

◆ A design for a solution that is believed to address all of the user requirements.

Deliverables

The following deliverables are required:

◆ One or more examples of the desired project outputs that have passed all the required tests.

◆ Test procedures and equipment that can be shown to be able to distinguish between compliant and non-compliant solutions.

◆ Test results demonstrating performance in line with requirements.

◆ Documentation showing which single final version of the design is capable of passing all the tests.

◆ An updated plan for the implement phase incorporating all relevant new information.

Responsibilities

Sponsor

The sponsor has a continuing responsibility to ensure that the funds and resources allocated to the project are well spent and are kept in line with the anticipated business objectives. This will involve monitoring progress reported in the weekly reports from the project manager against plan, and intervening to protect the project investment if required.

The sponsor's specific roles during the build and test phase may involve reviewing and approving test documentation to acknowledge that the test procedures and results are acceptable on behalf of the firm.

Project manager

The project manager is responsible for:

- Planning the activities and managing the work against the plan.
- Managing the critical chain: tracking progress, and taking management action when appropriate.
- Reporting progress.
- Allocating tasks to individuals and ensuring co-ordination between all tasks.
- Ensuring that whatever is built can be demonstrated to correspond to what was designed, and that proper records link different versions of the design, the hardware and the test procedures used.
- Ensuring that the test procedures are adequate for showing that the project outputs are fit for purpose and that the final test results provide sufficient proof of the system capability.

Team members

As during the design phase, team members should:

- Ensure that they have a satisfactory understanding of the tasks they have been asked to do. This involves not only clarifying the technical nature of their personal deliverables, but also clarifying what inputs to use, what to do with their individual deliverables once they are available, and when the deliverables should be produced.
- Execute the tasks assigned by the project manager, taking responsibility and authority within the agreed boundaries of each task.
- Report progress, problems and concerns to the project manager in a timely manner. This may mean telling rather than waiting until asked.
- Acknowledge that responsibility for project success is held jointly by the project team, and this means that team members should support each other actively rather than have each individual working only for their own benefit.

▶ Programme board

The programme board will:

◆ Intervene to take corrective action on projects on an exception basis, using the information provided in the programme summary reports.

◆ When necessary, change the prioritization of the projects in the firm's portfolio to reflect new information. This may mean that existing projects are upgraded, and have better access to resources, but it may also mean that existing projects are downgraded. If this happens, then the affected project may lose resources with obvious schedule implications.

▶ End-user representative

End-user involvement in the test phase is normally essential for the success of the project. This is obvious in the case of public trials, but there is also great benefit in having the end-user representative agree that internal tests are sufficient and that a solution that passes the tests will be acceptable. The end-user representative may also witness or take part in key tests and should sign off the final version of the design.

▶ External suppliers

External suppliers carry the same responsibilities as team members. However, as they usually run their internal activities as projects in their own right they often have additional responsibilities to generate and validate test procedures that they use internally before their deliverables are handed over for incorporation into your project.

▶ Process

The plan for the build and test phase should have been updated at the end of the design phase, so that it accurately reflects the workstreams implied by the design. It is normal to take a step-by-step approach during this phase, building and testing progressively larger parts of the final design so that when the whole thing is integrated there is high confidence that each of the parts work. Getting these steps right is one of the areas where project planning requires a deep understanding of the technical area, since the task breakdown will be very closely matched to the structure of the design. What follows is a general description of a build and test phase of a technology project. For other sorts of project, the structure will need some adaptation but the general principle of proving parts of the solution separately before trying to prove the integrated solution should still apply.

If your organization has an ISO 9000 or equivalent quality system you will probably already have a set of guidelines and procedures for creating hardware and testing it to confirm that it fulfils requirements. Since such procedures will already have been tailored to suit your organization you should of course use them.

Fig. 10.1 Build and test phase process flowchart

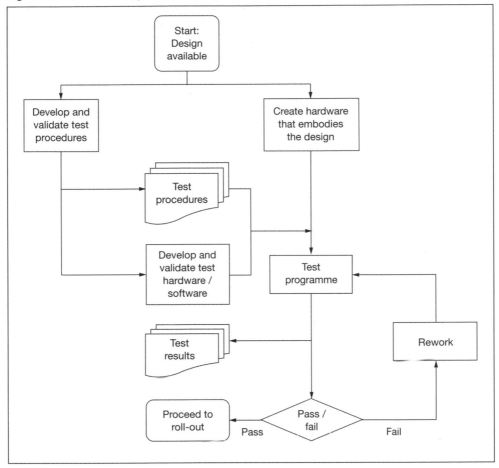

The general idea with the build and test phase is that whatever is built should reflect what was designed (since the design was driven from user requirements) and tests should show that user requirements are satisfied. The final series of tests on the whole solution should demonstrate that every user requirement has been met, but for tests on parts of the design there may be only an indirect linkage to user requirements. Since it is rare for each user requirement to match exactly one part or sub-part of the design, the process of inferring a suitable test for individual components requires some skill.

Key to the build and test phase is the requirement for tests to produce adequate proof of acceptability (see Fig. 10.2). This may seem trivial but only to those who have not yet managed a programme subject to strict requirements of proof. In most situations where the project output will be used outside the company, or will be used inside the company for things that affect our costs or risks, we need high confidence in the solution before it is rolled out. The solution must be not only adequate, it must be proved to be adequate. So the testing must be done in a way that minimizes doubt, and this involves establishing a logical chain between the system under test and some other system in which we already have confidence. The tests mean nothing unless they show how the system compares to some trusted reference. The first block of work for any of the tests is to set up this logical sequence.

Fig. 10.2 Build and test programme sequence

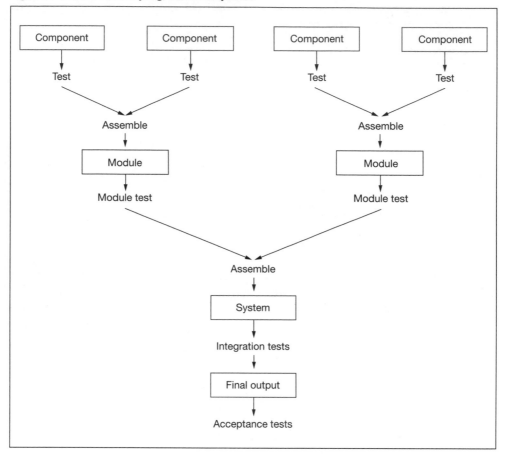

The basic process for developing a meaningful test programme is as follows:

◆ Work through the user requirements and decide how each item can be demonstrated or proved. This is the point where you will be grateful that you took such care to quantify and bound each of the user requirements during the define phase. For component-level or module-level tests, inferring an appropriate test will involve working down through the design from the user requirements to the specific performance requirements of the module.

◆ For each item, write a test procedure that calls for the system to be exercised under circumstances that correspond to the situation implied by the user requirements, and specifies what constitutes a pass or a fail result. Do not forget that the real-life environment is often messy, but users will have assumed that they will be using the system in just such circumstances. So some of your tests must show that the solution works as intended not only in the laboratory but also in a real or simulated user environment. Further tests will need to show that the solution not only works but does so reliably in such an environment. This is why it is normal to conduct field trials as well as laboratory tests before launching a product. Recreating the uncertain conditions of the real world in a repeatable way is difficult, and it is harder still to prove that the degree of uncertainty recreated in your tests faithfully replicates the uncertainty in the real world. In some fields, one must rely on the statistical and simulation skills of third-party test houses to ensure that internal testing is sufficient.

◆ Set up test hardware and software to provide controlled inputs as called for in the test procedure, and to record results systematically. It is essential that any systems used for this purpose are themselves trustworthy. It must be possible to show that the inputs they generate are what we intended to apply to the system, and the outputs they record are the true outputs of the system. Hence the test hardware and software must usually be itself tested.

At each stage of testing, a failed test generates useful information: it shows us what the problems are. The appropriate response to a test failure depends on circumstances, but it is not always appropriate to go back and modify the design and hardware immediately. This is because it may be important that all tests are conducted with the same version of the hardware, and it may also be possible to roll up the modifications that address several issues into a single design change. The project issues log is a good way to track and record possible design changes until a decision can be made about how to deal with them as a complete set.

At the end of the build and test phase, the project output should be ready for users, and there should be signatures on a sign-off document to say so. With such confirmation in hand, the project manager can now update and re-issue the implementation phase plan, knowing exactly what the finished project output looks like and what this means for the roll-out process.

? Ten key questions: build and test

1. Is the project under control? Are activities, progress, expenditure, changes and risks being managed?   Yes/No

2. Do the tests provide evidence that each of the requirements listed in the user requirements document has been met?   Yes/No

3. Do testing, measurement and observation procedures establish a direct link between the things being tested and trusted references?   Yes/No

4. Do the tests give adequate confidence that *the design* will not only work, but does so with acceptable reliability?   Yes/No

5. Do the tests cover what happens when the user does something wrong, or tries to use the design for a purpose that was not included in the original requirements?   Yes/No

6. Do the tests cover not only the requirements that users were able to describe explicitly, but also those that were implicit (e.g. ease of use, recognition of brand markers etc)?   Yes/No

7. Do the tests replicate the conditions that the design will encounter in the hands of users?   Yes/No

8. Can you prove that the single version of the design that you are proposing to roll out to users passes all of the tests (as opposed to several versions of the design, each of which can pass some but not all tests)?   Yes/No

9. Given the consequences of failure and the costs of corrective action during or after roll-out, do the test results give sufficient confidence that such failure will not happen?   Yes/No

10. After the design and the plan have been updated to reflect the information that emerged during testing, do the anticipated business benefits of the project still outweigh the remaining costs?   Yes/No

implement and review

1
2
3
4
5
6
7
8
9
10
11

What is the implement phase?

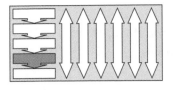

As many project managers have learned to their cost, creating a fully-tested product or service model is only half the battle. In order to realize the business benefits, the project outputs must be put in the hands of users who then do things differently in a way that helps the business. Occasionally, this can be done easily just by distributing the project outputs to users. However, project benefits often depend on getting users to change their behaviour in some way (even to make things easier for them), and this means that the implementation phase often tests a project manager's communication, negotiation and persuasion skills to the full.

Objectives

The objectives of the implement phase are to:

◆ ensure that the project outputs are adopted by the business;

◆ secure the business benefits so that they will persist after the project has finished.

Scope

In scope	Out of scope
◆ Two-way communications with users and other stakeholders to get buy-in and make the roll-out process work smoothly. ◆ Training and support of users and those who will be providing ongoing support. ◆ Replication/distribution of project outputs, and resolution of associated issues.	◆ Adding new features or enhancements in response to user comments (note them for a possible follow-on project). ◆ Continuing support for a new business process. ◆ Tackling strategic or regulatory barriers to adoption that have emerged during the project (these should have been identified as emerging risks and escalated through the sponsor earlier in the project).

Starting inputs

The following inputs should be available:

◆ A signed, re-confirmed PID giving authority to spend on the roll-out.

◆ Validated new product and/or process that is known to conform to user requirements.

◆ Implement phase plan updated with the best information available at the beginning of the phase.

Deliverables

There should be one main deliverable at this stage in the project:

◆ A finished project, with users using the outputs and delivering business benefits, and no longer depending on the project team for support. (Note that though the core deliverables of the project may be completed in this phase there may be other activities after handover in the review phase.)

Responsibilities

Sponsor

The sponsor retains responsibility for project supervision and focus on business benefits throughout the project. At the end of the implement phase the sponsor may take on line management responsibility for the newly-created product or service. Even if the project outputs fall completely or partially outside the sponsor's area of normal responsibility, the sponsor is nevertheless responsible for ensuring that the outputs are adopted and supported by appropriate managers.

Project manager

The project manager is responsible for:

◆ Planning and managing project activities.

◆ Monitoring and reporting progress against the plan.

◆ Ensuring that business benefits are delivered.

▶ Team members

As during the design and test phases, team members should:

◆ Ensure that they understand their own tasks and how they fit into the overall project.

◆ Execute their tasks, using initiative to solve problems by themselves within the boundaries of their delegated authority, and to escalate other problems up the management chain.

◆ Communicate effectively with the project manager and other team members about progress, problems and risks.

▶ Programme board

The programme board will:

◆ Monitor project status and intervene if required.

◆ Manage the firm's project portfolio continuously to keep returns optimal. This may mean occasionally raising or lowering the priority of individual ongoing projects.

▶ End-user representative

The role of the end-user representative depends on circumstances, but includes:

◆ Acting as a lead user or champion among the user community.

◆ Taking on sub-project manager responsibility for some of the handover activities.

◆ Signing off the project to acknowledge that the team have delivered.

◆ Acting as a trusted intermediary in negotiations with user groups who may, for whatever reason, believe that what is being delivered does not meet their needs.

▶ External suppliers

Suppliers who have been part of the development team retain their responsibilities as team members (see above). However, during the implementation phase it is possible that these suppliers, or other external companies, will also take on responsibilities for ongoing support of the finished project output. Such responsibilities probably fall outside the scope of the project, but defining these responsibilities and negotiating the support contract may well form part of the project.

Process

Fig. 11.1 Implementation phase process flowchart

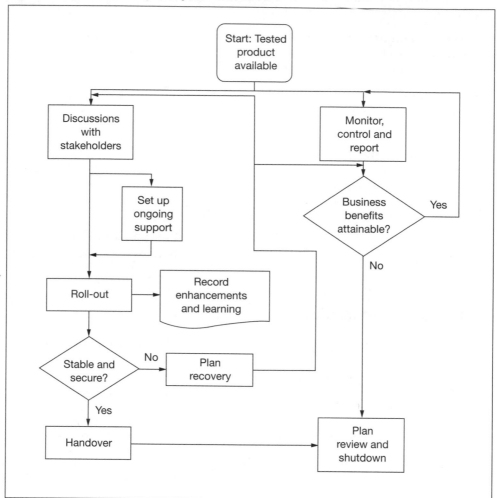

The implementation phase can start when there is a final version of the project output available, and approved funds to pay for the roll-out. This last point explains why companies usually spend so much effort in the definition, design, build and test phases, trying to find out what the users really want and making sure that what is produced corresponds to it. It is not unusual for the cost and time of a roll-out programme to exceed the cost of all the previous phases put together several times over, and it is essential that the product or process that is rolled out is the right one (see Fig. 11.2). The exact cost of the process or of each copy of the product will not be known until the design is tested and signed off, and so funding for the roll-out may be contingent on the results of the build and test phase.

Fig. 11.2 Typical project spend profile

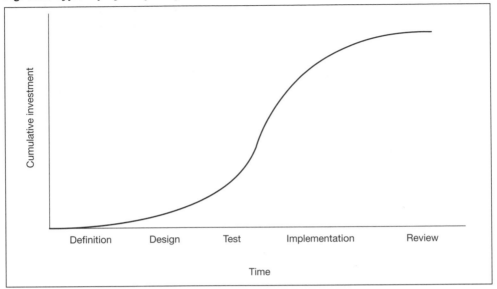

Communication with those who will have to take on the project outputs once the project is complete is key to successful implementation. This group probably includes users and support staff, but may include their customers or managers and any other stakeholders. Such communication should have been taking place regularly throughout the project, but becomes more intensive as roll-out draws nearer.

As always, communication should be two-way. People need to learn about the new product or process, but they should also be able to talk about their needs for the timing and style of the roll-out process, and for subsequent ongoing support.

> **!**
>
> ### Common sense
>
> One of the most frustrating experiences for a project manager is to take a project all the way through to implementation and to discover that, despite everything that had been said about the need for the project, the users just don't want it. They might even actively or passively try to oppose the roll-out. This does not happen every time, but when it does, it is important to handle such resistance properly.
>
> The first step is for you, the project manager, to realize that such resistance is not evidence of either malice or stupidity – though it might seem that way. It is just some people's way of coping with change. What you are asking people to do is change their behaviour in some way. Most people have developed ways to rationalize or to justify their current behaviour to themselves, and even if your proposed change would benefit them, their logic will drive them to oppose you. Someone who is opposing you can almost certainly give you a seemingly rational explanation of why this is the right thing to do. Remember also that the benefits of your project for the business may be great, but that individuals may be materially worse off, for example through a loss of authority or a change to less interesting work. Such fears are powerful and entirely reasonable, but unless you probe for them you will not discover that they underlie some of the other objections, since many people are afraid that voicing such concerns will make them appear selfish.
>
> So you must talk with people and understand what is actually happening. Your next action must depend very much on what you have heard. You still have the option to announce 'Do it this way because the boss says so', but before you adopt this approach, think carefully about whether this is in the long-term interests of the firm. Lateral thinking can sometimes suggest a solution that will allow the objector to retain their self-respect while removing the barrier to adoption of the project.

There are many possible launch or roll-out approaches. Products can be launched globally simultaneously, or country-by-country over a period of months. Processes can be switched overnight, or they can be run in parallel for a transition period. The best approach depends on the details of the markets and the technology and resources involved, but there should have been a reasonably clear idea of how roll-out would be done in the earliest versions of the project plan, during definition.

During roll-out, there are sure to be many issues and suggestions that arise when the project's output is put into the hands of users. Of course, some of these suggestions will need to be addressed immediately, but it is important that all suggestions are handled in a controlled way and not allowed to disrupt the roll-out. Keep the project issues log up to date, and keep applying the change control process. It is normal for a project to generate several suggestions for further projects, and these should be captured and handled as proposed projects rather than added to the current one. If these are taken on by the original project, they will extend the scope, time and cost of the original project and will of course stimulate their own spin-off projects – so the original project will continue for ever! This is one way to lose control of your project and miss your original target date by a long way. Record ideas that do not fit within the scope of the current project so that they can be reviewed later.

Implementation work is subject to problems for a whole range of possible reasons. Any problems need to be managed as soon as they become apparent. A recovery plan may involve repeating some or all of the earlier steps and, given the high costs of the implementation phase, this can jeopardize the commercial viability of the project even at this late stage. Time and money that has been spent cannot be recovered (it is sunk), whereas money we have yet to spend could be spent elsewhere. This means that if a project is found not to be viable then the firm might be better off abandoning it even if it has got all the way through to implementation (see Fig. 11.3).

Fig. 11.3 Sunk costs and decision making

Imagine that you want to make a journey from A to B. You set off from A, but after a while you realize that you have drifted off the straight line A–B, and you are at C. What is the only relevant question to ask at this point?

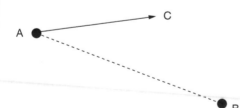

Most people would agree that the answer is 'How do I get from C to B?'. The distance A–C has already been travelled, but as long as you really want to go to B, you ignore your recent journey A–C and concentrate on whether it is still worth getting to B.

This is quite easy with the points A, B and C in a triangle, but many people believe that different rules apply with project spending: they don't. If a project drifts off track, then at any particular moment the only question is whether the benefits as we now expect them outweigh the costs from where we are today. If we discover the benefits are much further away than we thought, then it does not matter how much we have spent so far, it only matters that the benefits might not be justified by the remaining costs. Only taking into account time and money already spent will lead you to throw good money after bad.

?

Ten key questions: implement

1 Does the roll-out plan embody realistic assumptions about whether users will change their behaviour as desired when presented with the project outputs? Does it allow enough time and effort for communication and building buy-in? Yes/No

2 Can the roll-out plan be adapted quickly to cope with different scenarios such as negative publicity or rapid competitor response? Yes/No

3 Will key development and test staff continue to be available during roll-out to cope with emergencies, even though they may be taking on roles on other projects? Yes/No

4 Are adequate records being kept of who has received what? Are these in a format that is compatible with our other systems, with regulatory requirements, and with continuing efficient operations? Yes/No

5 Are users now routinely using the project outputs without problems? Yes/No

6 Is there explicit agreement from the end-user representative that handover is complete? Yes/No

7 Will the business benefits continue to flow once the project team is disbanded? Are there named individuals who are ready, willing and able to take on responsibility for ensuring that benefits continue? Yes/No

8 Have the success criteria established during the definition phase been met? Yes/No

9 Is the project issue log clear? Yes/No

10 Are there clear reasons to extend the project (e.g. if business benefits can be enhanced further) and that justify keeping the project team together rather than handing over to a suitable line department? If so, has the proper scope management procedure been applied? Yes/No

What is the review phase?

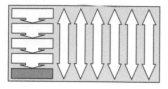

The review stage is not about delivering the project outputs, but it is nevertheless, something that organizations do to ensure that recorded project costs cover everything involved in the project rather than being hidden elsewhere. It is also the main formal mechanism to try to capture useful learning from projects so that future projects work better, and so is the key to the continuous improvement process for projects.

Objectives

The objectives of the review stage are to:

◆ ensure that everything set up or created specially for the project is properly shut down so that no further costs are incurred and resources can be allocated to other tasks;

◆ capture what was learned during the project so that it can benefit the organization as a whole;

◆ review opportunities for enhancements to the project deliverables, or unrelated spin-off projects, and decide how to deal with them.

Scope

In scope	Out of scope
◆ Returning hired or leased equipment. ◆ Decommissioning facilities, test hardware and software. ◆ Archiving for future project reference and possible regulatory purposes. ◆ Reviewing project with users, team members and other stakeholders.	◆ Enhancements or support of primary project deliverables.

▶ Starting inputs

The following inputs are required at this stage of the project:

◆ Shutdown plan.
◆ PID with authorization to carry out review phase work.

▶ Deliverables

The following deliverables are required:

◆ All recurring costs which were incurred purely on behalf of the project shutdown.
◆ Project file archived.
◆ Post-implementation review report.

▶ Responsibilities

▶ Sponsor

The sponsor's main interest in the project is the handover of the primary deliverables at the end of the implementation phase. However, they have a continuing responsibility during the review phase to protect the commercial interests of the firm by ensuring that the project gets properly shut down and does not leave behind lingering costs.

The sponsor will also review the project and decide which of the suggested spin-off projects should be turned into a proposal.

▶ Project manager

The project manager's main responsibilities are the same as earlier phases though the detail is different:

◆ Planning and managing project activities.
◆ Monitoring and reporting progress.
◆ Ensuring that the project is truly finished and shut down.

▶ Team members

Team members will still have tasks to do during the review phase. They will still need to understand those tasks and execute them as before. They will also be called upon to take part in honest and open discussion of the project so that as much as possible is learned from it.

▶ Programme board

Though the review phase should be short and there should be little opportunity for the project to drift far from the plan at this stage, the programme board will still expect to see regular reports and will intervene if required. It will also review suggestions for spin-off projects presented in the normal way as PIDs for approval.

▶ End-user representative

The end-user representative is often a source of learning about their experiences of the processes used to distil user needs and turn them into a new product or process. This viewpoint on these issues needs to be recorded just as much as that of the project team.

▶ Process

Fig. 11.4 Review phase process flowchart

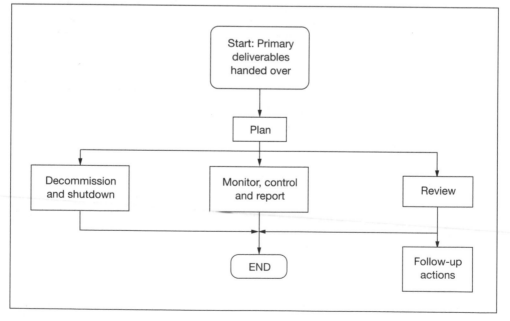

There are examples in many companies of equipment that was hired for use on a project but not returned at the end of the project. This equipment continues to incur costs indefinitely until someone investigates why the bills keep arriving. Since the project has by then been shut down, it usually takes days of effort to confirm that the equipment is no longer needed. This is wasteful, especially since it would have taken only a few minutes for the right person on the project team to phone the supplier and get the equipment taken away if this had been done during the project.

Planning the decommissioning of project infrastructure requires as much care and attention to detail as planning any other block of work. It is important to remember that this is the last chance you will get to use the knowledge and records built up during the project; there will be nobody left to answer queries or sort out what to do with bills after you have finished this phase. Other people will not necessarily know which of the records you created must be kept for safety or regulatory reasons and which can be destroyed. It would be much more expensive for someone else to analyze the project records than for the project team members to do the analysis using what they already know.

As always, once the plan has been created, the work to execute the plan should follow on easily.

The review phase is so named because it should always include a project review, even if there are no shutdown tasks. The project review involves at least two main activities: information gathering and recording. The information gathering can be done as a series of conversations or interviews, and it is usually a good idea for the project team to hold a review meeting so that different points of view can be shared. A review meeting should be carefully organized as there is a natural tendency for people to try to use such meetings to apportion blame or justify their own actions. The core of the session should be directed at answering a small number of basic questions:

◆ What worked well, and why? What should we therefore do more of?

◆ What did not work well? Was this truly bad luck or were there danger signs or prior experience that were ignored? What should we do less of?

◆ What is the best information currently available about the scale and type of business benefits which have actually resulted from the project? How does this compare with the original business objectives? With the benefit of hindsight, what should we have done during the project to minimize the negative differences and maximize the positive ones? What general lessons does this give for future projects?

◆ Were there points in the project that felt critical but weren't? Were there points which we now know were critical but which we did not realize at the time? What does this tell us about our use of available information, and what can we do differently to improve our decision making?

◆ How will we disseminate this knowledge so that other people in the firm can benefit from it?

Note that all of these points are directed towards 'what can we learn?' rather than 'who is to blame?'. These questions are fundamentally different, but real learning will be hard to achieve if people who may have simply made an honest mistake feel that they have to defend their actions rather than talk about how such mistakes can be avoided in the future.

The review meeting is also a convenient forum to discuss some of the suggested spin-off projects, since the people involved should have a good feel for what might be involved in them.

The last task on the project is to write and submit the post-implementation review report.

Ten key questions: before you start

1 Do the users, the new process owners, support teams or any other stakeholders have all the information they need to carry on using the project outputs?   Yes/No

2 Has all the documentation (and, if necessary, hardware and electronic data) been indexed for easy retrieval and archived?
Does the archiving procedure comply with regulatory or statutory record-keeping requirements relevant to the project outputs?   Yes/No

3 Have all equipment rental and service contracts associated with the project been cancelled and final bills settled?   Yes/No

4 Have the desks, computers and office space used by the project team been cleaned and the relevant people notified so that they can be re-allocated?   Yes/No

5 Has everything that will not be re-allocated or archived been dumped? (Beware that hazardous or confidential material will need specialist treatment.)   Yes/No

6 Have all staff costs, supplier invoices and internal cross-charges been processed and the project accounts closed?   Yes/No

7 Have you gauged the extent to which the original objectives were achieved? Have you examined the changes in costs and revenues of the relevant departments and estimated the true business impact of the project?   Yes/No

8 Have you reviewed the project with the team, stakeholders and company management?   Yes/No

9 Have you passed on learning from the project to team members, company management and other project managers?   Yes/No

10 Have you recorded your learning about your own project management skills?   Yes/No

Appendix A
the critical chain method

This book presents the critical chain method of managing projects. This has been shown to deliver great benefits over other techniques, but it differs significantly from other project planning and management techniques. It may be a new way of working even for some experienced project managers. For this reason, the key points of the technique are summarized here.

The critical chain method evolved from work by Eli Goldratt on improving factory efficiency.[1] Goldratt advocated identifying the bottlenecks in production and concentrating all effort on ensuring that these stages in the production process worked at maximum efficiency, thereby maximizing the efficiency of the overall process (this was an application of his theory of constraints). Goldratt applied and extended this work in the domain of project planning and management, and this led to the critical chain method.[2]

Understanding activity durations

When a project is planned, most of the activity durations have to be estimated, and the actual durations of those activities may differ from the original estimate (see Fig. A1). Critical chain provides a means not only to retain control in the face of such uncertainty but also to exploit it.

One of the problems with the uncertainty of task durations is that the variability is predominantly positive: tasks often take longer than the estimate, but are very rarely shorter. There are several reasons for this:

◆ It is well documented that most people do not fully apply themselves to a task until at least half of the allowed time has elapsed (sometimes known as 'student syndrome'). This is entirely normal, and people may subconsciously or consciously allow for this behaviour in their original estimate. But it means that by the time the real work starts, there is often only just enough time left to complete the work package as it was originally understood, and the slightest problem is enough to push the duration beyond the deadline. Hence there is a tendency for tasks to be completed late no matter how much time is allowed.

◆ When several workstreams merge together into a single dependent activity, that dependent activity cannot start until the last of the merging workstreams has finished. Thus, even if three out of four merging workstreams have finished early, the downstream tasks will start late if the fourth workstream finishes late. All project workstreams must eventually merge together to produce the deliverables, but the fact that only the worst workstream matters means that project duration is again much more likely to be late than early.

◆ Parkinson's Law[3] states that work expands to fill the time available. On projects, people hardly ever report that a task is completed early, even if their work was of acceptable quality long before the deadline. People may assume that there is some duty to spend the allotted time on the task or they may be tempted to add additional refinements to make the work better, or they may delay delivering the completed work until the deadline because they know that they will be given more work to do if they signal that they are available. Hence project managers rarely get the benefit of tasks being completed early.

Fig. A1 Activity merge bias

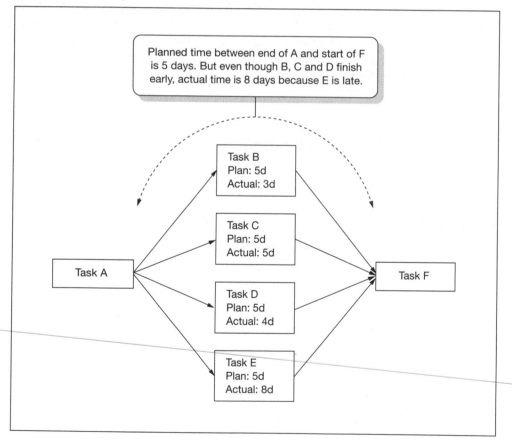

Critical chain and activity durations

Critical chain addresses these biases in duration distributions both by addressing the behavioural causes and by turning the variability in task timing to our advantage by exploiting the statistical properties of sequences of uncertain events.

A manager applying the critical chain method will avoid student syndrome and Parkinson's Law by avoiding emphasizing a fixed delivery date when assigning tasks. Team members are rewarded if they can show that they have delivered as quickly as possible instead of being motivated to deliver on a particular day.

Using classical methods of estimating task durations, the true likely duration of each and every task gets padded with an allowance to prevent embarrassment: unless otherwise directed, most people will give an estimate of the time in which they are almost certain to be able to complete the task, whereas the average time it will take is usually shorter. This protects the estimator because they thereby reduce the chance that they will later be shown to have underestimated. Of course, for the reasons outlined above, the work normally ends up running until the deadline, even though task deadlines include this hidden padding.

Aggregating contingency

The second consequence of task estimates including contingency is that it is an extremely wasteful way to apportion contingency time. The statistics of linked processes are such that it is much better to aggregate the uncertainty into a single pool for the whole project rather than try to protect tasks one by one (see Fig. A2).

Fig. A2 Buffers on each task

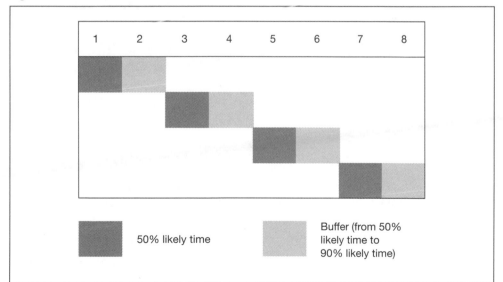

50% likely time

Buffer (from 50% likely time to 90% likely time)

Consider four tasks in series, which have each been estimated to take two weeks to complete. In fact, we know that the two-week estimates are probably the time by which the tasks are 90% likely to complete, and further probing of the estimators reveals that there is a 50% probability that each task can be completed in one week. So the classical estimating method would give a chain of four two-week tasks, for a total of eight weeks.

Using critical chain, we build the plan using the one-week estimates, in the full knowledge that each of these is only 50% likely to be true, to give only four weeks in total. We allow for the uncertainty by adding a 'project buffer' which is shared between all four tasks (see Fig. A3). However, from statistics (see 'Statistics of aggregating tasks' below) we know that the uncertainty of this buffer duration is less than the sum of four individual one-week buffers. We can achieve the same overall level of protection for the project by having a two-week aggregate buffer as we did by having four one-week individual task buffers. So our critical chain plan is only six weeks long overall instead of the eight needed when each task had a buffer, and the two-week saving is due only to taking the buffers away from individual tasks and aggregating them into a single buffer for the project as a whole. Critical chain can shorten a project by over 20% in this way, with commensurate cost savings, without increasing overall risk. This may seem like black magic to project managers trained in other methods, but it is true.

Fig. A3 Project buffer

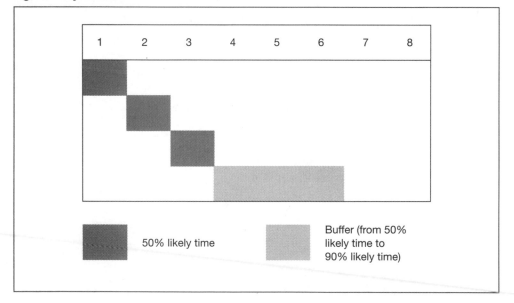

Statistics of aggregating tasks

The amount of uncertainty in a number is expressed mathematically as its standard deviation, σ. It is also common to use variance, σ^2, which is just the square of the standard deviation. If several uncertain processes are aggregated, then the overall variance is the sum of the variances. This is important because if the uncertainty of each number rises linearly, the uncertainty of the aggregate rises much more slowly (with the square root). For example:

If four numbers each have a standard deviation of 2, then each has a variance of $(2^2 =)$ 4. The sum of the variances is $(4 \times 4 =)$ 16, and the standard deviation of the aggregate of the four numbers is $(\sqrt{16} =)$ 4. Treating each of the numbers separately would face us with a total uncertainty of $(4 \times 2 =)$ 8.

The statistics of combining many uncertain events also work to counteract the biases which make individual tasks more often late than early. The Central Limit Theorem shows that, no matter how skewed the distributions of the durations of individual tasks, the distribution of the aggregated uncertainty will tend towards the symmetrical normal distribution as the number of tasks rises. In other words, the overall project stands a reasonable chance of coming in early, even if individual tasks have a long tail on the late side! (See Fig. A4).

Fig. A4 Skewed distribution for single task

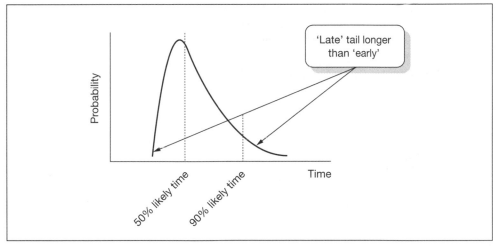

▶ Focus on critical activities

Although critical chain can add much value in planning a project by handling uncertainty more efficiently, it is in helping managers to understand and focus on the critical activities that it has the greatest day-to-day impact during a project.

Because the name critical chain sounds similar to critical path it is tempting to think that they are the same. The critical chain includes all the critical path activities, but whereas the critical path is defined only by task dependencies, the critical chain is defined by both task dependencies and resource dependencies. In other words, it recognizes that the minimum time to complete a project can be driven as much by the limited availability of resources as by task sequencing. Activities not on the critical path can form part of the critical chain if they rely on resources which are in demand elsewhere, and any change in their duration has an impact on the project duration. Much of the thrust of the critical chain method is directed towards protecting the critical chain: anything that affects the critical chain affects the project. The key techniques of critical chain are feed buffers, resource buffers and eliminating multitasking.

▶ Feed buffers

Non-critical activities must never be allowed to impact the critical chain. This might happen, for example, when a critical chain activity depends on a non-critical activity that suffers a delay. Critical chain inserts a feed buffer between the non-critical workstream and the critical chain task, so as to insulate the critical chain from the uncertainty in the non-critical workstream timing. This feed buffer is calculated in the same way as for the project buffer, but covers only the tasks on the joining workstream (see Figs A5 and A6).

Fig. A5 Distribution for aggregate tasks

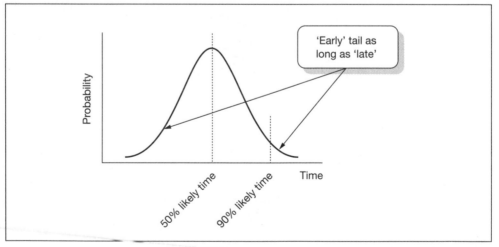

Using feed buffers to protect the critical chain from the non-critical activities frees the project manager from having to use early start scheduling. (Early start scheduling means starting all activities as soon as possible, even if they are not critical.) During the early days of a project it is often better not to be distracted by having to start many activities at once, and project managers should focus on the critical chain activity that starts the project.

Fig. A6 Activities merging onto critical chain

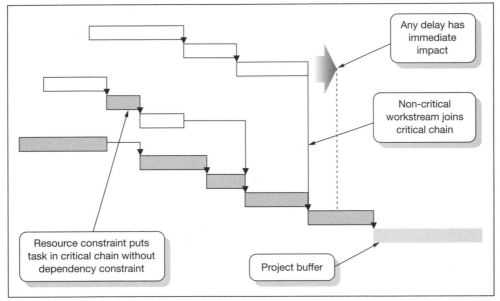

Any delay has immediate impact

Non-critical workstream joins critical chain

Resource constraint puts task in critical chain without dependency constraint

Project buffer

▶ Resource buffers

The critical chain activities must always have all of their resources and inputs available as soon as the preceding task finishes. The simplest form of resource buffer is a reminder flag in the project plan to re-confirm resource availability before the start of each task. When the project depends on another project to release the critical resource on time, it is necessary to include a real buffer period between the tasks on each project. Resource buffers can even take the form of spare or standby staff who are deliberately not assigned to other activities, or, in the case of sub-contract suppliers, cash payments for holding their own staff on instant availability.

▶ Eliminating multitasking

The strict discipline of the focus on the critical chain requires that people should not try to do two tasks at once, especially if one of them is a critical chain activity.

In Fig. A8, all three activities are delivered simultaneously through multitasking, but if resources are allowed to prioritize and do one task at a time, two of the three tasks are delivered early and the third no later than through multitasking.

Fig. A7 Feed buffer

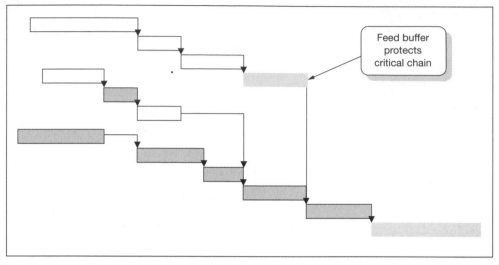

Feed buffer protects critical chain

Fig. A8 Multitasking

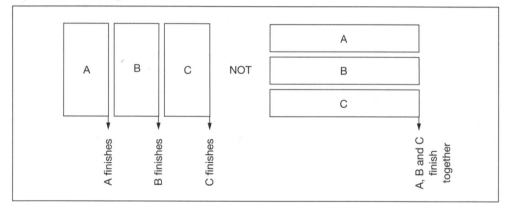

▶ The project buffer as a diagnostic

During the critical chain planning process a project buffer is created at the end of the project and feed buffers are created to separate critical tasks from non-critical ones. During a project the current state of these buffers is an easily-understandable shorthand for the status of the project. It is to be expected that projects will often use some of the buffer (after all, the original task duration estimates were only 50% likely times), but managers should take action if it seems likely that all the buffer will be used, since this means that the project will be late overall.

Fig. A9 Buffer usage and project status

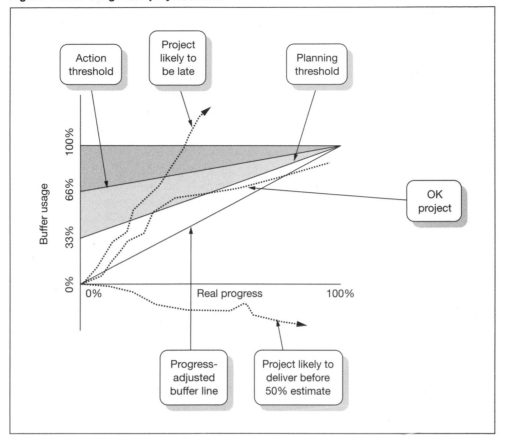

The danger level of buffer usage depends on how much work there is still to be done: 40% buffer usage would be a serious warning sign on a project which is only 15% complete, but is probably not a problem on a project which is 85% complete (see Fig. A9). As a rule of thumb, a project manager should:

◆ plan recovery actions if the buffer usage exceeds one-third of the progress-adjusted buffer (this is the total buffer scaled by the proportion of work remaining to be done); and

◆ enact the recovery plan if progress-adjusted buffer usage is greater than two-thirds.

> ## Action summary

> ## Planning

The basic requirements are:

1 Create the project structure in the normal way. Pay attention to risks, and take care not to miss out any activities: team members won't have any slack time from task-level contingency time to pick up any extras that are discovered along the way.

2 Gather estimated durations for each task. Start by asking for the time for 90% confidence of success – this is the time most people will give if unprompted. Then ask for the time for which we would only be 50% confident of success (make clear that you fully expect half of these estimates to prove to be low, and you will not regard this as a mistake on the estimator's part).

3 Set the task timing in the baseline plan using the 50% estimates.

4 Allocate resources to tasks and identify the critical chain using both task dependency and resource constraints.

5 Add a project buffer calculated using the aggregated differences between the 50% estimates and the 90% estimates.

6 Add feed buffers to isolate the critical chain from non-critical workstreams. Schedule non-critical workstreams as latest-start rather than earliest-start, so as to make it easier to focus on getting the project up and running at the start.

7 Add resource buffers as required to ensure that critical resources are available when required.

> ## Executing

The basic requirements are:

1 As always: work the plan.

2 Assign tasks to named individuals, but avoid giving exact deadline dates unless absolutely necessary (to meet an externally-driven timetable, for example). Instead insist that tasks should be completed as soon as possible.

3 When monitoring progress, expect that 50% of tasks will overrun the 50% likely time, and 50% will finish early. Try not to criticize any team member whose task overruns – as long as they started as soon as they had the necessary inputs, they worked 100% on the task (without multitasking), and they passed on their outputs as soon as they were available. Similarly, make clear that you expect tasks that are completed early to be handed over early, so as to get the benefit of positive variation.

4 Use the resource buffers to ensure that critical resources are never idle or unavailable.

5 Monitor usage of the project buffer against actual progress made to determine the true status of the project. Plan for recovery when buffer usage exceeds progress by more than 33%, and enact the recovery plan if buffer usage exceeds progress by more than 66%.

6 Monitor usage of feed buffers to warn of possible impact of non-critical work-streams on the critical chain, and take pre-emptive action before any such event.

Notes

1 *The Goal: A Process of Ongoing Improvement*; Eliyahu M. Goldratt; North River Press Publishing Cororation; ISBN: 0884270610; 2nd rev. edition (1992)

2 *Critical Chain*; Eliyahu M. Goldratt; North River Press Publishing Corporation; ISBN: 0884271536; (April 1997)

3 For those seeking an entertaining read that nonetheless makes some telling observations about real organizations, see C. Northcote Parkinson's *Parkinson's Law*, 2002, Penguin Books

Appendix B
classic planning and progress measurement tools

Evidence shows that the critical chain method of structuring and managing projects on which this book is based can deliver great benefits. But it is difficult to implement the full critical chain method if you are the only one in your organization doing so. Many project managers will find themselves having to use other methods simply because of their organization's standard procedures. Those using the widely accepted critical path method will still find that most of the content of this book is applicable, but that there are differences in planning and project status monitoring and control techniques. What follows here is an overview of the most common critical path/PERT method. This represents the classic viewpoint without reiteration of the weaknesses of this approach that have been amply addressed elsewhere in this book.

▶ Critical path and PERT plans

Plans for projects run using the critical path method start the same way as every other plan (see 'Planning process', page 81). Clarify user requirements, identify activities using both top-down and bottom-up analysis, establish dependencies, and create the project structure on either a Gantt chart or a network diagram (PERT chart). The differences come in the areas of estimating, task scheduling and allowing for uncertainty.

▶ Estimating

Obtain an estimate of effort (or duration if it is a fixed-duration task) from someone who has been properly briefed about the requirements for each task on the plan. Most people will instinctively protect themselves by giving a safe estimate, and so these figures can be built into the project plan with confidence that the estimated time for each task is secure.

If the full PERT method is followed, then the estimating procedure is slightly more involved. Rather than take a single safe estimate for each task, ask for three estimates: an optimistic estimate, a most likely estimate and a pessimistic estimate.

These three data points are used later to give an estimate of the aggregate uncertainty in the project.

▶ Critical path scheduling

With estimates for the effort required for the various tasks, it is possible to use project planning software to identify the critical path. The critical path is the longest chain of dependent activities in the plan, and hence it sets the minimum project duration.

Fig. B1 Path durations and critical path

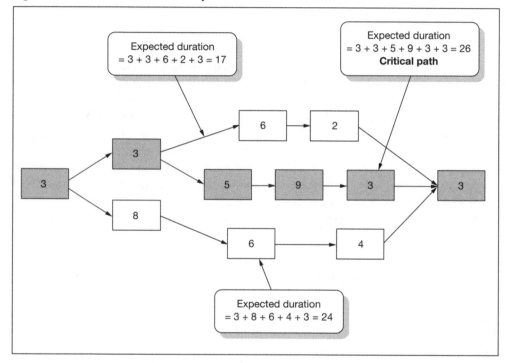

In Fig. B1 there are three possible paths through the project network, with total durations of 17 days, 26 days and 24 days. Since all tasks have to be done in order to finish the project the minimum project duration is 26 days and the 26-day path is the project, critical path. The other two paths have some slack time (2 and 9 days respectively for the 24-day and 17-day paths, representing the difference between their respective path durations and the duration of the critical path). The critical path has zero slack: every activity on the critical path must follow the preceding one without delay otherwise the project will be delayed.

The estimated time for completing the above project is 26 days, but this is subject to some uncertainty. Knowing the critical path, the project manager can focus effort on keeping the critical path activities moving without delay. But it is not safe to ignore the other activities. If, for example, the first 8-day activity on the 24-day network branch suffered a 4-day delay, then the actual duration of this branch would become 28 days. This is two days longer than the duration of the critical path in the original plan, and so the delay in a non-critical activity can cause the critical path to jump to a different part of the network (see Fig. B2). If this happens then the project manager must quickly re-prioritize activities to minimize the chances of further delay.

Fig. B2 Effect of actual times on critical path

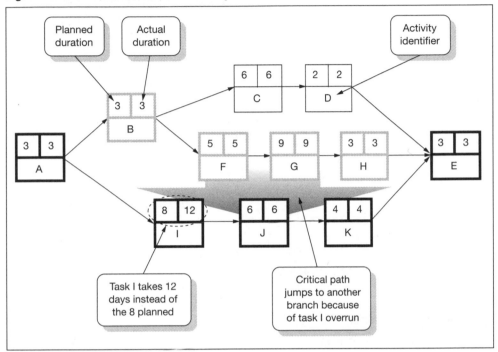

The fact that the critical path is not fixed makes the project manager's job much more difficult. One of the usual ways to reduce the chances of the critical path jumping to a different branch of the network is always to start all tasks as early as possible, irrespective of whether there is slack in the plan that would theoretically allow the task to be delayed. If earliest-start scheduling is used, then the whole of the slack period is available to absorb time overruns in non-critical tasks before the critical path is affected.

▶ PERT: Allowing for uncertainty

The difference between basic network diagrams and the full Project Evaluation and Review Technique (PERT) is in the way that they handle uncertainty in task estimates. By accounting for the uncertainty in each task estimate PERT provides valuable insight into the likely variability in duration of the overall project, and hence provides better information about what completion date is realistic.

The possible range of durations of each task is expressed as a probability distribution. There is a variety of possible distributions but in practice there are only three that are commonly used: triangular, rectangular and normal.

For each type of distribution, the shape of the distribution is set by the optimistic, most likely, and pessimistic task duration estimates.

Triangular distribution

Fig. B3 Triangular distribution

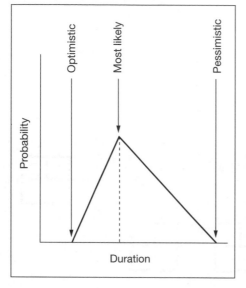

It is common to find that the optimistic estimate is not much shorter than the most likely estimate, but that the pessimistic estimate is much longer. Hence the estimated distribution is skewed. The triangular distribution is a convenient way to represent this. It assumes that there is a negligible chance that the duration will fall outside the optimistic and pessimistic limits, and that probabilities vary linearly between these limits and the most likely duration. These assumptions may be wrong but they are a lot easier to use than the alternative of guessing a shape for the distribution curve. Since the plan probably has many different uncertain activities the detail of distribution for each activity is not usually terribly important and a triangular distribution is an easy compromise.

Rectangular distribution

Fig. B4 Rectangular distribution

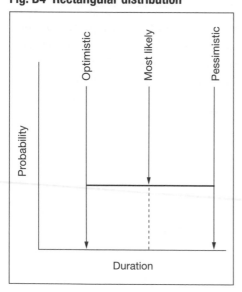

Sometimes estimators may not know a most likely time, or the estimates of most likely time from different estimators may vary widely even though they agree on optimistic and pessimistic times. If this happens, then you can use a rectangular distribution instead of the triangular distribution. A rectangular distribution is equivalent to saying that we know that delivery will occur sometime between two dates, but that we do not have a feel for when.

Normal distribution

Fig. B5 Normal distribution

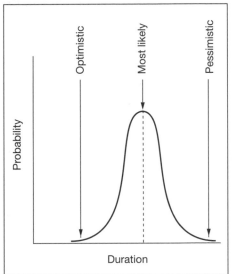

Many real-world processes have been found to have what is termed a normal distribution. The term normal implies a statistical distribution with certain well-defined properties. Among these is the fact that it does not have clear upper and lower limits. The probability of any particular duration becomes very small for durations far from the mean, but it never becomes zero. This is appealing since there is always a slim chance that something bizarre will happen and the task will take far longer or far shorter than anticipated. In consequence, the optimistic or pessimistic times must be interpreted as the times that the task has only a 5% chance of exceeding.

Another significant property of the normal distribution is that it is symmetric around the mean. The pessimistic time is as far above the mean as the optimistic time is below. In the absence of real data on task timing this might be a reasonable assumption, but it is more common to assume a distribution with a longer tail on the pessimistic side.

▶ Planning with variable task timing

The benefit of the PERT technique is that it gives insight into the impact of task timing variability on project timing. This can be done either with some basic statistics or by simulating the project.

Statistical rules of thumb

When PERT was developed, the following statistical relationships were found to apply to the distributions of timings of individual tasks:

$$\text{Expected task duration} = \frac{\text{Optimistic} + (4 \times \text{Most likely}) + \text{Pessimistic}}{6}$$

$$\text{Task variance} = \frac{(\text{Pessimistic duration} - \text{Optimistic duration})^2}{36}$$

Variance is a statistical measure of the amount of uncertainty in a number. Tasks with greater duration variance have a larger spread of possible timings. Use the expected duration of each task to construct the project plan, giving the expected duration of the overall project and allowing the critical path under expected conditions to be identified. The variability of the overall project is assumed to be that of the critical path:

Critical path variance = Sum of variances of tasks on critical path

The standard deviation σ of the project duration is simply the square root of the variance:

$$\text{Standard deviation of project duration } \sigma = \sqrt{\text{Critical path variance}}$$

Knowing the expected duration and the standard deviation of the duration it is possible to calculate the probability that the project will finish within a certain time. For example, it is often useful to know the time in which we can be 95% confident that the project will complete. Normal distribution tables or a spreadsheet show that this value is found by adding 1.64 times the standard deviation on to the expected duration (see Fig. B6).

Fig. B6 Range of possible project durations

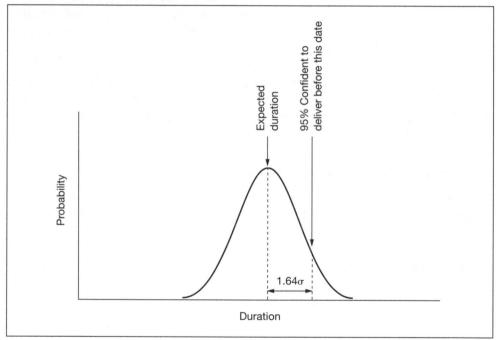

Presenting project timing information in this way is a very powerful argument to resist pressure from management to commit to delivering the project at the expected duration time. The expected duration is only 50% likely and the time required for 95% confidence of delivery is significantly longer.

Project simulation

The statistical rules of thumb are powerful and can be implemented on a spreadsheet even if your project planning package does not support PERT. But they do not allow for the fact that variability in task timings might make the critical path change. If this happens then the calculations of project duration will be working with the wrong sequence of tasks. If you have access to a Monte Carlo simulation software package, or if you have the patience to create a Monte Carlo simulation model in a normal spreadsheet, you can overcome this problem.

A Monte Carlo simulation is a simulation of the project repeated many times so as to build up a picture of the average variability. In each run of the model the duration of each task is chosen randomly according to the distribution parameters estimated for that task. The model should include all of the task dependencies and so some tasks will be delayed by others just as in the real project. After many hundreds of simulations the observed distribution of simulated project durations will give a fair idea of the probability distribution for the overall project timing, including changes in critical path and whatever task distribution functions you chose to use. Such information is sometimes essential to inform discussions during planning and project definition but remember that when you run the real project it will only have one duration, not a distribution.

Progress measurement

The simple and intuitive means of updating a Gantt chart to show actual progress to date (see page 71) is entirely applicable under the critical path method. When updating a plan always remember to update not only the work that has been done but also the work still to do on each task. This will prevent you from being misled about your true rate of progress.

An updated Gantt chart is an excellent tool for a project manager, but it is not so good for answering senior managers who ask 'How is the project going?' These people expect a terse summary, and they are likely to reply to a list of tasks and revised dates with 'OK, but what does that mean? Are we ahead of schedule or behind?' When some of your dates are ahead and some behind this can be an awkward question to answer concisely. Fortunately, there are some standard metrics that can be applied to summarize the status of individual tasks and of the overall project. These are the earned value, the schedule performance index and the cost performance index.

▶ Earned value

Each task in the project adds value in some way. Earned value analysis assumes that the value created is in proportion to the planned effort, and so small tasks add proportionally less value than large ones. It is easy to think of examples where this is clearly not the case, but any other method would be fraught with difficulties over assessing the relative value-add of different sorts of task. At any one time through the life of the project the notional value that has been created is proportional to the percentage of the project that is complete:

$$\text{Earned value} = \text{Budget} \times \text{Percentage complete}$$

The original project budget is used in order to get to a value in pounds or euros. If the project is complete then 100% of the budget value has been created, whereas if the project is less than 100% complete a proportionally smaller fraction of the budget can be claimed.

Project budgets are usually made up of a number of external purchases plus a charge for the time internal staff are expected to spend on the project. If there are no large external purchases then the budget is dominated by the cost of staff time and so the assumption implicit in the earned value approach that value creation is proportional to effort will hold true. But if the project budget contains large items of capital expenditure then costs are not proportional to effort. Earned value can still be used under these circumstances, but the schedule and cost performance indices will need to be interpreted with care. Some organizations therefore prefer to exclude external purchases when calculating earned value.

▶ Schedule performance index

A key question for a project is where it stands relative to the schedule. This question could be rephrased as 'How much of the progress we should have made to date have we actually made?' The schedule performance index is defined as:

$$\text{Schedule performance index SPI} = \frac{\text{Earned value}}{\text{Planned spend to date}}$$

Strictly, this calculation is the answer to the question 'How much of the value that we should have created to date have we actually created?' but the earlier assumption that progress, value and spending are proportional makes these questions equivalent.

It may seem strange that schedule performance is measured in proportion to spending, but planned progress is related to planned spending provided that the project is charged for the time people spend working on it.

A schedule performance index below 1 indicates that the project has made less progress than planned. An SPI figure above 1 means that the project has made more progress than planned.

▶ Cost performance index

Project managers and sponsors are also usually interested in project costs. With good recording of the cost of staff time and committed spending it should be possible to get a good picture of actual costs at any time through the life of the project. But this only shows what has been spent, whereas what people usually want to know is whether spending is higher or lower than what had been planned. Rather than relate actual cost to that planned to date, the cost performance index relates actual cost to earned value. This means that the index is not skewed if a project runs late but still spends what was originally planned. The CPI is the answer to the question 'How much of our spending to date is justified by our progress?' It is defined as:

$$\text{Cost performance index CPI} = \frac{\text{Earned value}}{\text{Actual cost to date}}$$

Just as with SPI, figures below 1 are bad, and those above 1 are good. A CPI of less than 1 means that the project has so far cost more than can be justified by progress, and vice versa.

Appendix C
managing large and complex projects

The techniques described in this book are generally applicable and will add value when applied intelligently to any project. In order to make the material more directly applicable it has been necessary to present it in a framework with certain assumptions about the size of the project and the sort of organization involved. One of the key assumptions was that the project would be relatively small and simple. Large projects (those with many thousands of tasks and hundreds of people) are disproportionately more difficult to manage. With so many activities and dependencies, the probability that something will go badly wrong is higher, and the time the project manager can devote to each area of the project is lower. Large projects therefore make much more use of formal checks, intermediate levels of management, and rigorous adherence to procedure.

An alternative approach to this book would have been to try to create a framework that could be applied to any project no matter how large. This is the approach adopted by the UK Central Computer and Telecommunications Agency with their PRINCE 2 methodology. PRINCE 2 has gained wide acceptance outside the UK and beyond its original area of software development because it is a rigorous all-encompassing framework. It is an excellent complement to the practical guidance provided in this book, and its wide acceptance makes it a good starting point for anyone who needs to manage large projects or those of such complexity that the project life cycle framework described in this book is not helpful.

For those working in a PRINCE 2 environment it may be helpful to see how the elements of PRINCE 2 align with the topics covered in this book. Figures C1, C2 and C3 show the PRINCE 2 template and how its elements match the sections of this book.

Fig. C1 The PRINCE template

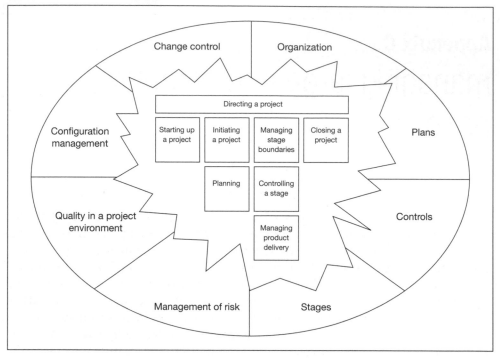

Fig. C2 Fit with PRINCE components

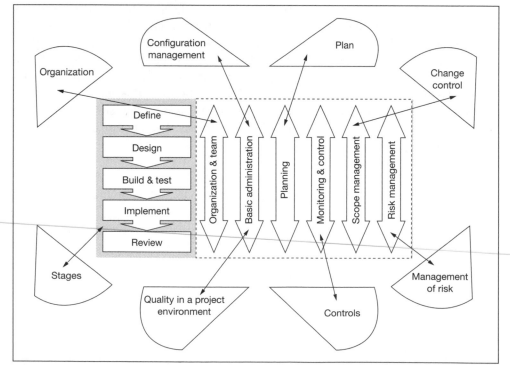

Fig. C3 Fit with PRINCE processes

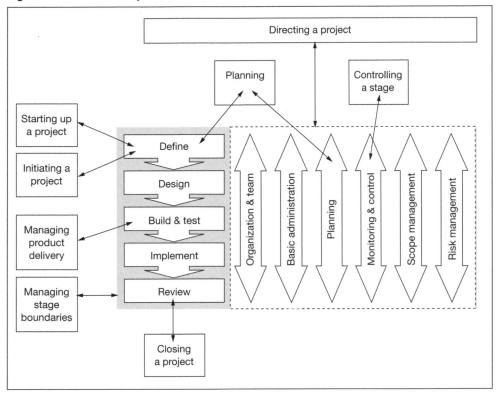

Appendix D
project planning software tools

There are a great many project planning tools available, and all of them claim to be able to help you to manage projects better. The software producers like to call their products project management software rather than project planning software, as though their software can manage a project automatically. It can't. That does not mean that the software is useless – there are many situations where a good software tool is vital – but it does mean that nobody reading this book should be under any illusions that buying a particular piece of software will make all their projects run smoothly.

The area of project management where software support is invaluable is in project planning and tracking progress. The relationships in an average project plan are so complex that nobody could plan and re-plan a project quickly enough for the information to be current unless a support tool is used.

This book will make no attempt to list all the various software tools available, far less make any recommendations. Different organizations have different requirements and different project managers will emphasize different aspects depending on their level of experience, and so it is inappropriate to make recommendations here. What follows is a brief overview of the capabilities of software used to support project planning and progress tracking. More information and reviews describing many of the available packages can be found on the Internet.

Planning software can be categorized into two groups. The first supports planning and progress tracking of a single isolated project. This book concentrates on the task of managing a single project and even this is a complex job. However, many projects have to run in organizations that have many projects running at once. In these situations there may be resource contention not only within a project but also between several projects. The second type of project planning software adds capabilities to support planning and progress tracking in an environment where several projects are running and events on one can affect the others.

Tools for single projects

Data entry and planning

The basic requirements are:

1 Look for an easy and intuitive interface. You will be too busy to be able to spend much time learning a new package. In some ways, it is more important that a package should be easy to use than that it should have sophisticated features (of course the ideal is both), since it is important that the software should be used rather than investigated and put away.

2 It should support work breakdown structure, Gantt charts and network diagrams. Ideally, it should be possible to enter the tasks in any one of these formats and then have the package translate the representation into the others as required. It is easiest to specify task dependencies using drag-and-drop links on a network diagram, but it is also useful to be able to edit the links by changing the task identifier numbers in the rows of a spreadsheet.

3 It should allow groups of tasks to be rolled up so that low-level detail can be hidden when looking at the overall project structure.

4 It should be possible to specify task durations as either fixed or variable. For fixed-duration tasks it should be possible to enter the effort required.

5 It should be possible to specify the effort required for a variable-duration task and to assign resources to the task so that the duration is calculated automatically. Note that tasks often require work from several resources, and the task duration should be the time taken for the slowest of these to complete their work.

6 Resources should have cost information associated with them so that the plan includes the cost of people's time. Ideally, providing this information should be a basic function of the package rather than something that the user can search for with a custom query of the project database.

7 The software should automatically identify resource over-allocation and should provide a resource-levelling tool. Ideally, this should have various settings so that the project can be optimized in different ways (e.g. minimum time, minimum cost, minimum resource loading and so on).

8 The software should be able to identify the project critical path and should optimize its resource levelling in order to minimize the impact on the critical path.

9 If you wish to use the critical chain method, then it is a good idea to look for software packages that support this. The calculation and insertion of buffers can be done manually using other packages, but it is much more convenient if this is automated.

▶ Progress tracking

The basic requirements are:

1 All software packages should allow you to enter the actual progress on tasks while preserving the original timeline for comparison. Some will allow you to save multiple versions of the timeline so that you can then compare several options for the plan.

2 All software should allow you to set the project start or end date, and should also allow you to specify today's date (the 'as-of' date). This is useful if you want to see the status of the project at some date in the past.

3 Some software will automatically calculate progress metrics on tasks and on the project as a whole. This is a useful feature, but you should make sure that you understand exactly what numbers the software is using in its calculations.

4 On large projects the process of gathering information about time usage and task status is laborious, and unless the software makes it easy to update the plan there is a danger that this task will be left aside. Some packages can be integrated with timesheet software that may already be in use in your organization, and others have timesheet features themselves.

5 It is helpful for team members to be able to see the current status of the project against the plan. If everyone has a copy of the planning software and has access to the file then this is quite easy, but it is also expensive to provide multiple copies of the licence and it introduces the risk that the plan might be changed accidentally. Some packages have been designed to overcome these problems by providing an Internet-type interface. Depending on the details of the package, this might allow the sponsor or other internal stakeholders to view the current plan on the company intranet. It may also allow team members working off-site to view the plan and even enter data about their own tasks.

6 Some software packages can be set to generate automatic e-mails to team members to tell them of their tasks. This might be helpful under some circumstances, but it introduces the risk that team members might receive conflicting instructions.

▶ Tools for multi-project environments

If a project is running in isolation, then the data regarding the project can be stored locally on the project manager's computer. This means that the software is not obliged to deal with data that might be stored in several locations and might be updated by several people simultaneously, and so it can be relatively simple. If there are several projects running simultaneously in the organization then it is quite possible for each to use a separate package in this way. This is a common approach and it relies on the various project managers and resource managers co-ordinating and negotiating so that resources are properly managed. As the number of projects increases, this method becomes increasingly difficult since the co-ordination task becomes very complex. Some project planning software packages offer a partial solution to this problem by running a company-wide resource pool and allowing planners to resolve resource contention not only within a single project but also across the whole firm. Making this system work relies on strict adherence to the procedures for time recording and updating availability information, but it can produce significant gains in resource utilization. The gains are greatest where there are groups of people with interchangeable skills, since project planners can then choose alternative resources in the case of resource contention.

As well as using a central resource pool, some multi-project software tools can roll up the status of several related projects to create summaries of multi-project programmes for the programme board or other senior managers. Some packages also allow the programme board to assign priorities to each project that is authorized. This is a very useful feature since it can provide an unambiguous decision-making rule that the software can use when deciding how to resolve resource contentions between projects.

glossary

Activity   In project planning an activity is a clearly bounded piece of work, with clear inputs and outputs. Everything that happens on a project should be part of an identified activity.

Buy-in   Commitment to the project and its outputs from others in the firm – particularly among the users, who will need to devote time and effort to adopting the project deliverables. Getting user buy-in is one of the most critical project success factors.

Central Limit Theorem   Well-proven statistical theorem showing that the distribution of the means of other distributions tends towards the normal distribution (even if the other distributions are non-normal) as the number of means increases. So even if the distribution of possible timings of each individual task is heavily skewed, the distribution of timings of a project (a large number of tasks treated together) will be symmetrical.

Change management   Change management can mean one of two things, so be careful that the person you are talking to means the same thing as you. It can mean the management of organizational change, including handling the people issues associated with changing the way people work. It can also mean recognizing and managing changes to the definition of the project – what is referred to as scope management in this book.

Cost of capital   Rate of return on investment demanded by the investors in the firm. All activities undertaken by the firm should produce returns at least equal to the cost of capital: if they do not, then they destroy investors' value.

Critical chain   The sequence of activities that defines the minimum project duration once realistic resource constraints are applied. It includes critical path activities and also activities that compete with the critical path activities for resources. The name also applies to the planning and management methodology that underpins much of what is described in this book.

Critical path   The longest chain of dependent activities in a plan – defines the shortest possible project duration in the absence of resource constraints. The name also describes a project planning and management approach that focuses on the critical path activities – note that the critical chain methodology is significantly different.

Deliverable   A clearly identifiable output of a project or project activity.

Delivery team   The group of people responsible for delivering the project. The project manager and the team members.

Dependencies   Logical relationship between project activities which means that one cannot be completed (or sometimes cannot be started) before the other.

Discount rate   Analogous to an interest rate, and used to adjust the value of future or past cash flows to their present-day value.

Drum resources   Those project resources which are critical of the limited availability, such that their avoidability limits project progress. So-called because "the project marches the beat of these resources' drum".

Duration   The elapsed time required to complete a task. Some tasks have fixed durations, but it is usually a function of the effort required and the number of people available to work on the task.

Effort   The amount of work involved in completing a task. Commonly measured in man-days.

End-user representative   The day-to-day user contact for the project.

Feed buffer   Buffer time inserted between a non-critical task and a critical chain task, in order to limit the impact of delays in the non-critical activities on the project.

Gantt   Timeline view of project plan. Can be updated to show both planned and actual state of progress.

Hurdle rate   Minimum rate of return on a project investment demanded by some companies.

IRR   Internal rate of return. The rate of financial return on the money invested in a project.

Network diagram   A graphical means of showing project structure, with emphasis on the dependencies between activities.

NPV   Net present value. The sum of all positive and negative incremental cash flows resulting from the project discounted to their present-day value. A project with a positive NPV should be undertaken, whereas one with a negative NPV should not.

Output   The product or result of a piece of work.

Payback period   The amount of time needed for the incremental benefits generated by the project to pay back the money invested in it.

PERT   Project Evaluation and Review Technique. Methodology for project planning using network diagrams with multi-point estimates of task effort to allow for uncertainty in task estimates.

PDD   Project Definition Document.

PID   Project Initiation Document. Single document setting out what business benefits the project intends to produce, how these will be created (i.e. the plan) and what the costs will be. Forms the basis of project authorization.

Programme   A co-ordinated group of projects that together change the organization in ways that support strategic objectives.

Programme board   Responsible for the approval, prioritization and monitoring of projects across the organization.

Project   'A set of co-ordinated activities, with a specific start and finish, pursuing a specific goal with constraints on time, cost and resources.' (ISO 8402)

Project buffer   The aggregated uncertainty of all the tasks on the project, collected together and inserted between the last activity and the safe project completion date. Aggregating the uncertainty in this way allows the safe delivery date to be protected with much less total buffering than if each task was buffered individually.

Project execution   Carrying out the work in the plan.

Project manager   Individual responsible for planning, co-ordinating, tracking and reporting progress of a project, and to whom project team members are responsible.

Resource   Facilities, equipment or people used in executing the project. Since people are by far the most common constraint, the word resource is often used interchangeably with person.

Resource levelling   The process of adapting the plan to resolve resource contentions and ensure that resources are not over-stretched or double-booked.

SMART   Specific, Measurable, Achievable, Realistic and Timed objectives for delegated tasks.

Sponsor   An internal buyer for a project. The sponsor asks for the project to be set up and will use its output. The firm provides the sponsor with a budget and a project team in order to create the anticipated business benefits, and the sponsor is responsible for ensuring that these benefits are actually realized and money well spent. Hence, sponsors act as project supervisors.

Work breakdown structure   An indented list showing all the activities on a project, on which sub-tasks can be rolled up into larger blocks. Total effort on the project can be found by summing the effort for each task on the list.

index

FT Knowledge
FINANCIAL TIMES

Professional Training
in
Project Management

FT Knowledge and *Project Value Associates* have joined forces to deliver project management training courses using the tools and techniques in this book.

FT Knowledge provides public courses, day and evening, in New York, London and other major cities around the world. They also provide in-house courses tailored to the needs of your organization and a variety of project management training and professional development material.

Organizations who have used our training courses include organizations of all size from the following sectors:

- retail finance
- wholesale finance
- engineering
- construction

- land and property
- law
- defence
- telecomms

- IT
- regulatory
- publishing and media
- capital markets

Courses are suitable for all levels of experience and all levels of executive:

- project managers
- analysts
- managers

- directors
- project sponsors
- technical staff

- consultants
- professionals
- operations staff

The training courses aim to **make** your life as a project manager easier. This means:
- ✔ increasing the chance of a successful project,
- ✔ showing you how to use project management tools and techniques in real-life situations,
- ✔ giving you a chance to discuss real project issues with the experienced project managers who are your tutors and with others on the course,
- ✔ reducing the stress in your job.

For more information contact:

finlearn@ftknowledge.com
www.ftknowledge.com
+44 (0)20 7010 2508

enquiries@ITVA.Net
www.ProjectValue.com
+44 (0)20 7588 5544